Voyage to America:

The Journals of Thomas Cather

VOYAGE TO AMERICA

The Journals of Thomas Cather

Edited with an Introduction by
Thomas Yoseloff

Illustrated with Contemporary Drawings by
HARRY TYLER

NEW YORK . THOMAS YOSELOFF . LONDON

Thomas Yoseloff
11 East 36th Street
New York 16, N.Y.

Thomas Yoseloff Ltd.
123 New Bond Street
London, W. 1, England

The illustrations will be found in a group following page 106

Manufactured in the United States of America

Introduction

Toward the end of January, 1836, Henry Tyler, who had just turned 23, walked the short distance across the fields to visit his neighbor and schoolmate, Thomas Cather. Both young men were bored: the shooting season was over, the charms of County society appeared pallid, and it would be several months before the fishing season was launched. There seemed little cheer in prospect for the winter months.

In the course of that afternoon's conversation, the two boys determined to travel to America. They had already made the grand tour of Europe, as every English (and Irish) gentleman of the day was required to do, and had traveled in Asia and Africa as well.

The decision was lightly taken in a spirit of high adventure, but travel to America in that time was not a light matter. Passage was dependent on the winds, and schedules equally erratic. The passage might take three weeks if the winds were fair all the way—but it might just as easily take six. Sailing vessels were ill-kept, crowded and uncomfortable; the food, as often as not, was just barely edible. The crossing was dangerous, and the casual traveler to America was not a common figure.

Fortunately the two young men did not give themselves time to weigh their decision carefully. Within ten days after their first conversation, they were aboard a vessel in Liverpool. We have no record of their preparations, but since they came armed with letters of introduction that opened the doors of the greatest houses in America—even the White House—we can assume that the few days were spent in working out itineraries, badgering family friends and local politicians, and "boning up" on the geography of the far reaches of the American territory, which must have been very far removed from the normal study of boys in comfortable Irish homes in County Londonderry in 1836.

The journal which Thomas Cather kept covers a period of eleven months, from early February 1836, when the two boys set sail from Liverpool, until their return in January 1837. While it does not have the depth of perception that characterized the more extensive journal kept by his French contemporary, Alexis de Tocqueville, Cather's journal is nevertheless a remarkable accomplishment. He was able to record in the most graphic terms the minute details of a journey of 12,000 miles which took him to New York, Philadelphia, Baltimore and Charleston, thence overseas to Cuba, back to New Orleans, up the Mississippi by steamer to Kentucky, by horseback, stagecoach and wagon into the depths of the American frontier, north into Canada, by vessel through the Great Lakes, and down the Hudson to Albany and back to New York. He found time to "see the sights" not forgetting the scenic beauties of Virginia and the Shenandoah Valley and the mighty Niagara Falls. He even penetrated by horseback deep into Indian country, venturing alone for a sojourn with the Pottowotamie tribes. This was not at all the sort of itinerary that might have been expected from a young man in his circumstances, and out of it emerged a diary that makes good reading more than a century later.

Young Cather was a good observer and an articulate recorder. His personal observations of the great statesmen of America — Andrew Jackson, Martin Van Buren, Henry Clay among them — were concise and outspoken. In his judgments he was often wrong — he could not believe that the states would remain united as the nation grew, or that America would not modify the democracy by instituting a landed aristocracy, which he deemed necessary to survival — but he was also amazingly right, foreseeing a quarter century before the event the inevitability of civil war over the slavery issue. He was blatantly intolerant of most Americans, their rough manners, their appearance, their hectic pace, their passion for money—in this he was aping the contemporary view of the educated European, a view that has survived in large part even to our times. But he was equally outspoken in his admiration for the strength of America, the concept of political liberties expressed in the Revolution, and the rise of the young Republic to a position of world power.

Thomas Cather's ancestors settled in County Londonderry early in the seventeenth century, acquiring landed properties in and near the town of Limavady (transcribed from the Gaelic *leam-a-vaddy*, leap of the dog). The family attained considerable local prominence as brewers, opened a bank, and became firmly established as a County dynasty. The Cather family became intertwined with the Tylers, another County family of considerable prominence. Henry Tyler, Cather's companion on his journey to America, married Cather's sister, and Thomas Cather's brother married Henry Tyler's sister.

A branch of the Cather family established roots in America, as did also the Tylers. Robert Tyler came to America in 1756, and after a brief career as a teacher, became manager of an iron foundry which today claims the distinction of being the oldest in the United States in continuous operation since the colonial period. Robert Tyler changed his name to Taylor, and the firm still bears his name, operating as the Taylor-Wharton Corporation.

The manuscript of the journal has remained in the family since it was written, and its publication has now been made possible through the kindness of Sir Henry Macdonald-Tyler, C. I. E. A brief portion of it was published in London in 1955, representing the first three months of the journal.

In publishing the journal in its entirety, it has been my purpose to present it essentially as it was written. I have undertaken a minimum of editing, changing spellings and punctu-

ation only when it seemed essential for clarity. For the most
part construction, punctuation and spelling—even in a few
instances obvious misspellings—have been left as they are, in
order to give the reader the flavor of the journal and a sense
of the conditions under which passages were written, as well
as the substance. The drawings reproduced in the book were
made by Henry Tyler, as an accompaniment to some portions
of the diary. Unfortunately, most of them were made in
Havana, and the most interesting portions of the journal are
not represented by Tyler's illustrations.

As for Thomas Cather, he returned to County Londonderry, where he studied the law and was admitted to the bar.
He does not, however, appear to have been very active as a
barrister. He became a member of the Royal Irish Academy and
devoted his life to scholarship. He had a deep and lasting interest
in the Gaelic language and Gaelic origins, and was noted for his
study of the Gaelic origin and meaning of local place-names.

THOMAS YOSELOFF

London, January, 1961

Voyage to America:

The Journals of Thomas Cather

February 1836

OWING to hard gales blowing from the Westward, we were detained several days in Liverpool, greatly to our discomfort. Not merely because Liverpool is a very dull place, but on account of the unpleasant state of uncertainty in which we were placed, not knowing at what hour we might start. But on Thursday, the 4th of February, 1836, the wind having shifted to the N.E., we were enabled to leave the dock, but had scarcely got our sails set, and were not more than two miles from Port, when a Maltese ran foul of us and carried away some of our rigging. In consequence of this misfortune we were obliged to put back to have the damage repaired. If one tithe of the curses that were launched against the Maltese had taken effect, he must have gone to the bottom, for deep and bitter were the maledictions which issued from our Captain and crew. Henry and I had been so much annoyed by having been obliged to go every day to the docks to ascertain when the ship would sail that we determined on remaining on board.

As people should always accommodate themselves to circumstances, and as the best philosophy in this world is to make oneself as comfortable as possible wherever one is, we determined to act on that plan, and to commence it that very day. The other passengers, having friends in Liverpool, went on shore to enjoy their society for another night. But we had few friends on English ground, our luggage was on board the good ship " North America," commanded by the tight Seaman Captain Dixey, and there our interest was, so we determined on remaining on board and making ourselves as comfortable as possible.

After having discussed the merits of a brace of fowls, and

11

seen the bottom of a flask of Champagne, we fell into a pleasant
and most edifying discourse on a great variety of topics, of
which speculations touching our future rambles constituted a
principal share. A bottle of Brandy, some hot water and sugar,
flanked by a copious dessert of choice fruit, were laid on the
table. The water in the jug was *fizzing hot*, the fire in the stove
was burning bright, the brandy in the decanter was sparkling
most invitingly, and the lumps of white sugar seemed almost
melting with desire to become more intimately acquainted
with the brandy. So we did as all men with any regard to their
own comfort would do, we pulled off our boots, cased our feet
in fur-lined slippers, for the night was very cold, drew our
chairs close round the stove, mixed each a glass of punch, and
having satisfied ourselves of the proper strength and flavour,
placed our feet on the fender, and whiled away the time by
laying plans for the future, an occupation that is so often
fruitless.

Retired to bed at a reasonable hour. Disturbed about midnight
by a most extraordinary noise, which commenced with a low
humming note then brisked up to something like a concert of
penny trumpets, and at last burst forth into a wild howling
dirge most terrible to hear. There was on board a Quadroon
woman, from the Island of Barbadoes, in the capacity of
Stewardess' assistant, named Tabitha Tapeworm, who had a
most inordinate affection for the brandy bottle. After we had
retired to our Cabin, she had got hold of the liquor which her
soul loved, and under its potent influence " kicked up the
bobbery " which so much startled us. In fact she fairly played
the Devil and broke things. However she made the amends
honourable next morning, apologized for the disturbance she
had occasioned, and assured us on her honour it should not
happen again. Next morning set sail.

16th. Hitherto we have got on very well, we are now upwards of a thousand miles from England, so considering the

season of the year we have no reason to complain. We have had some fresh breezes, with a heavy sea. My stomach has been in such a state of agitation as to prevent me carrying on this Journal, but the weather has now moderated, and as I was able to make a decent breakfast this morning on a mutton chop, I hope my squeamishness is over for the remainder of the voyage. I have had the pleasure of having had companions in misfortune, all the rest of the passengers have been equally sick, and that is a comfort. Sea-sickness forces one to acknowledge how much his happiness depends on the state of his stomach. Moralists tell us that a well-regulated mind is essential to happiness. That may be, but not more so than a well-regulated stomach. People little suspect how much the state of the mind and temper depends on the digestive organs.

When the wind is fresh and the sea rough, it is very amusing to see how the economy of the dinner table is disturbed. The soup is generally distributed more lavishly than is pleasant. Now a leg of mutton sidles up to a roast Turkey, then a large ham shows symptoms of getting alongside a boiled fowl, which, as if to make its escape, leaps from the dish and takes refuge in your breast, if you should happen to be sitting toward it. I have seen an apple dumpling get into motion at one end of the table, and in the twinkling of an eye bound along to the other end and deposit itself in the Captain's lap. It is also quite a common thing to see at the same time a decanter of Sherry hobnobbing with one of Madeira, and the Brandy flask coming to loggerheads with a bottle of Porter.

The other night, the second mate, a knock-kneed, round shouldered, shambling made fellow, with a drawling Yankee accent, came down into the Cabin. " Beg your pardon, Gentlemen," said he, " I want to get something out of the Medicine Chest." " Who's ill?" " Tom, Sir." (Tom was a black boy, who officiated in the Steward's Department.) " And pray, Mr. Perry, do you practise as Physician on board?" " Yes, Sir, I always

Physicks them as be sick." " What's your favourite prescrip-
tion?" " Oh! I be noways petiklar, I generally takes a few
of the things as comes uppermost." " And, what's the matter
with Tom?" " I'm sure, I don't know Sir, but he says he feels
rather petiklar queerish." " Well, Mr. Perry, don't spare the
Medicine chest on my account." " Never fear, Sir," said he,
laughing, " when I physicks a man, he seldom applies to me
again." " That is the case with the patients of a great many
doctors," said I.

The mate grinned, and proceeded to make up his dose. He
had a dirty tin can in his hand, into which he poured a very
ample allowance of Castor oil. After fumbling about for some
time, he took nearly a handful of Glauber salts and powdered
it over the oil, then a little Tartar Emetic, and stirred the
hellish compound with an iron spoon. " I'll be bound," said he,
" this'll settle Tom, it will work him fore and aft and make a
new man of him." " I'm afraid its effects won't be very settling,
Mr. Perry." " Never fear, Sir, I warrant I'll cure him." And so
the mate took his leave. I was curious to know how Tom stood
the dose, and next morning when I went on deck, I went forward and found him at the forecastle, leaning over the side,
with a most ludicrously woeful expression of countenance. He
had such a deep rooted despair, such utter hopelessness depicted
in his countenance, that one would have supposed that he felt
all was over with him in this world.

" Why, Tom," said I, in a commiserating tone, " what is
wrong?" " Ek, Ek, Massa," said the poor fellow, hiccupping
and grunting and with great difficulty getting out a word, " Ek,
Ek, Massa, dat dam Mate physic me so, me berry bad, berry
bad, indeed," continued he, shaking his head mournfully.
" Something pull my guts and all my inside up to my troat,
and then push dem down toder side. Ek, Ek, berry bad indeed."
And, in truth, he did look as if the medicine had done its work,
his face was curiously mottled over, of a pepper and salt com-

plexion, little of his eyes were visible but the whites, on his chin and breast was a broad streak which had manifestly been caused by the operation of the Tartar Emetic and one hand was laid expressively and sympathisingly on his stomach—it was a subject for Hogarth. After seeing Tom, I did not wonder that none of the Mate's patients ever applied to him again.

I think it is Dr. Johnson who defines a ship to be a prison with the contingency of being drowned. From this it would appear he had no love for voyaging. As to the risks attending a sea life, I do not think they are greater than those on shore, and to me there is a keen, pleasurable, excitement when it blows half a gale and the sea runs high as it has done the last week, to see the ship plunging forward like a courser from the spur, meeting and toppling the mountain waves that threaten to overwhelm her. And as she rises from the shock tossing off from her bows the water in a cloud of foam and spray, as a high mettled horse would champ and shake the froth from the bit, to hear the timber straining and the wind whistling through the rigging gives one an exulting sensation, and impresses one forcibly with the conviction of man's power, how he can make the most unstable elements to be the slaves of his will, and by his courage and skill can guide his vessel over the wild and lonely paths to its destined Port.

17th. Very light wind S.E. and by S. almost becalmed.

18th. Steady breeze from the East. Ship going eight knots. I find the time on board ship pass much more swiftly and pleasantly than I had anticipated. We breakfast at nine o'clock: I generally read three hours, spend the remaining time on deck till dinner hour at three o'clock,—after dinner we play a rubber of whist;—drink tea at eight o'clock—then a turn on deck, read for an hour or so, and to bed.

21st. For the first time since we left the Channel, we have seen a sail. The weather for the last three or four days has been very fine, mild and calm.

23rd. We are now on the banks of Newfoundland; a very sudden change has taken place in the temperature; yesterday the Thermometer stood at 56° — this evening it has sunk to 32°. The temperature of the water is still lower, this denotes the neighbourhood of an iceberg — a very unpleasant neighbour, by-the-bye. The weather is so thick we cannot see the length of the ship before us. We have, in consequence, altered our course, had an hour standing to the South. The Captain appears very serious and anxious — it is now past ten o'clock — I write this in my cabin before turning in — perhaps it is the last leaf of my log.

24th. Still afloat and safe from icebergs, owing to the alteration in our course, the Skipper thinks we are now out of their track — the thermometer has risen considerably.

25th. Sea smooth — Wind very light — Studding sails alow and aloft.

26th. Yesterday evening the wind freshened, then came on several squalls at short intervals and then it fairly set in to blow a gale. Awful tumbling during the night — this morning it still blows great guns. We are now bowling along under close reefed maintop sail and reefed foresail. The sea presents one of the most magnificent sights I ever witnessed — as far as the eye can reach is a confused tortured mass of roaring surges. The ridges of the waves are all roughened and broken into foam — while here and there an immense black billow, like a mountain in motion, comes sweeping on high over the other surges, till culminating to a lofty top, it tosses up a snow white cloud of spray, with a loud explosion. It was worth while coming so far to see the ocean in its angry mood. It has just struck eight bells (12 o'clock). Henry and I are the only passengers able to be up, the rest are in their berths groaning in agony of spirit. It is with difficulty I can write, everything movable in the cabin seems to be instinct with life, or rather to be possessed by a Devil — it was with no small trouble we managed to get breakfast over. During that repast, a pot of butter launched itself at Henry's head with the velocity of an arrow, a large piece of corned beef jumped off the table and bolted through the open door of one of the state rooms, with more agility than would have been expected from its corpulent appearance, and a dish of pork chops bounded off the board and set to jigging it on the floor very merrily. However we managed to get hold of some eatables before they all eloped. How we are to get through the dinner scene, I cannot imagine.

27th. Last night it blew tremendously hard; today the gale has increased, we are almost under bare poles. A ship on the weather quarter is lying to, about a mile distant. We just catch a view of her as she rises on the crest of a wave. The sea presents a most sublime spectacle — a howling wilderness of foaming waters — two of the sails have been blown to rags.

28th. The gale is gradually abating.

29th. Here is a change. The sea is quite smooth, and the wind almost fallen away. We are going now only at the rate of four knots.

March 1836

1st March. Come on again to blow very hard; the sea high.

2nd. Still blowing hard, and the wind right ahead, to use the Captain's phraseology, it blows a regular *tauteezer*, I guess.

3rd. Still blowing almost a gale. One of the sheep, in consequence of the rough weather, has died, greatly to the grief of Larry. Larry is an Irishman, and quite a character. He passed some years of his life fishing on the coast of Labrador; getting tired of that, he came to Liverpool, and entered this ship as a first rate seaman, but it was soon discovered that poor Larry knew as much of his duty as a pig does of navigation, so he was literally sent to the pigs.

He was installed in the office of stock feeder, he set about his work *con amore*, and applies his entire energies to fulfil the duties of his situation with credit to himself, and advantage to the animals under his charge. The cow stretches out her head and watches him with a wistful and affectionate eye as he walks about the deck. He seems to be on particularly good terms with the pigs, and the ducks, whenever he makes his appearance, salute him with an uproarious quack of welcome. Larry's head dress is of rather unique shape, it seems to be built after the model of a Mandarin's hat of ceremony, but during this rough weather he has doffed it, and mounted instead a woollen night cap. He is the most contented looking personage on board. All he has to do is to look after the stock. He has neither to go aloft, nor turn out at night to take his watch on deck.

4th. The weather again fine.

6th. A dead calm. Had a visit today from some of the crew of an American Whaler. Though about eight miles distant, the Captain sent a boat to us to learn the news from Europe. They had been cruising in the South Seas for 21 months and were returning home with a full cargo of oil, having killed 56 fish.

The United States are extensively engaged in the whale fishery. Ten thousand of their citizens are annually employed in this branch of commerce, which yields a very rich return — it is principally to the South Seas that they go. A ship is generally absent two or three years, combining the pursuit of fish with a trafficking trade with the natives of the islands. The port of New Bedford, and the little island of Nantucket, equip the greatest number of whalers. The inhabitants of the latter place are employed exclusively in the trade. According to the custom of the place every young man must go at least on *one* voyage and no youth dare aspire to the hand of any girl in the island till he has signalised himself by striking a harpoon into a whale.

Today a whale appeared close along side, and a shoal of porpoises — the sailors say the latter are attracted by the bright copper sheathing of the vessel.

8th. This morning on going on deck found we were just off Sandy Hook at the entrance to New York Bay. The sail from thence to New York is said to be very pretty in Summer, but at present the ground is deeply covered with snow, and consequently everything appears to disadvantage. Reached the city about five o'clock — went to Bunkie's — no room there, then to the City Hotel, where we have put up.

I have as yet said nothing of our fellow passengers: there were only three besides ourselves, an American, a Scotchman and a German.

The first, Mr. R., was returning home after an absence of three years, which he spent in making a tour of Europe. He has seen a great deal of the world, has read much, and is a very pleasant, intelligent man, but he is not a real American in feeling. He thinks the institutions of his country too democratic, he abominates General Jackson, and has a very unpatriotic attachment to England and every thing English. Every one has some peculiarity or other—the whim wham that possesses Mr. R. is that his digestive organs are deranged, and that every precaution is necessary on his part to prevent him falling a victim to dyspepsia. Accordingly he is, as he thinks, very careful in his diet; he eschews butter in every shape; for untoasted bread he has a most devout horror, but he eats four eggs for breakfast every morning, tucks in a very comfortable dinner, pies, puddings, etc., and winds up with a quantity of fruit and hickory nuts, enough to kill a pig. To procure exercise he practises every morning with a skipping rope, greatly to the edification of the sailors, and every evening before tea, he makes it a rule to laugh with all his might continuously for ten minutes at least, in order, as he says, to give due play to his lungs.

Mr. H. was distinguished by a very peculiar accent, a cross between the high Cockney and the broadest Scotch, and the German; a lee*tle* lee*tle* fellow, with all a German's love of trinkets, a gold chain round his neck, long enough and strong enough to hang him, and a bunch of huge seals to his watch, under whose weight he almost staggered. He is a gentlemanlike, and well informed person, and has come to New York to try his fortune in business. We are all here at the same hotel, and these same American hotels are curious places, vast menageries containing some very extraordinary animals, rare specimens of the human species well worthy the attention of the Naturalist.

The Americans appear to be essentially a locomotive people, they are continually on the move. The greater number transact their business in person, without the intervention of agents, consequently, there is always a crowd in motion to and from the principal marts. The hotels here are very numerous, and very large to accommodate the immense number of guests. At this hotel there are 150 or 200 persons who all mess together. At half past eight o'clock we have breakfast, at half past three we dine, half past six tea, and from nine till eleven supper is on the table. The Americans are great economists of their time, and in nothing do they show their despatch more than in eating. The first morning at breakfast I was absolutely astounded at the rapidity of their jaws. Homminy, Indian cakes and treacle, broiled fish, beef steaks, mutton chops etc., in " the twinkling of a bed post " were ravenously consumed, and before I had half finished my first cup of coffee the tables were cleared and I was left alone, like the last rose of Summer. But the feats at dinner were still more astonishing.

Day after we landed, went to see H. Hassan who did not know us. Insisted he never saw me before, and when we did make him " sensible " who we were, gaped with astonishment, and looked and looked again before he could find words to ask in the name of Heaven what had brought us there. Poor fellow, he looks wretchedly ill, and is most terribly Yankiefied.

Called on Mr. G., who also did not recollect me. Says I am greatly changed, so is he — Yankiefied too — not the person he used to be — looks like a man, whose whole attention is the making of money, and his whole study his ledger and day book. Asked us to dine with him on Sunday at two o'clock.

10th. Visited two museums, very good collections to the size. Called on Mr. Sampson, fine old gentleman, in bad health, engaged to spend the evening there. After sitting for an hour, took our leave, and walked about town. Visited one of the Law Courts. Lawyer making a " noration " in a drawling twanging voice; and the judge, honest gentleman, sat picking his nose, and yawning at the lawyer, and no wonder, for it was a very soporiferous speech.

Spent a pleasant evening at Mr. Sampson's — met there Dr. MacNevin, a fine animated, intelligent old gentleman, with a great deal of good, Irish feeling. Next morning he paid us a visit, which we returned, and had the pleasure of being introduced to Mrs. M. and the young ladies—engaged to spend the next evening there.

Walked about town seeing sights—by the bye, there is not much to be seen. Broadway (and why it is called *Broadway* I cannot tell) is the fashionable promenade of New York, it is nearly three miles long, and in some parts rows of trees line each side. It contains some good houses, but in general it is very irregularly built.

Sunday, dined with Mr. G.

Monday evening we spent at Dr. MacNevin's. The more I know the more I like him and Mr. Sampson, who, with his daughter, Mrs. Tone, was there to meet us. I had a great " palaver " with the two old gentlemen on Irish history and antiquities, and heard many stories of the men of '98. The two Misses MacN., pleasing, ladylike girls. One of the prettiest girls I have seen was a cousin of theirs whom we met there. We had music and singing, and spent a delightful evening.

Willard, the barkeeper, and one of the proprietors of this hotel, is said to be the most clever man in his line, in the United States. He keeps the books, and manages every department of this great establishment. His powers of memory are extraordinary. Every one, on coming to the hotel, enters his name, and the number of his room, in a book kept for that purpose, and if any enquiry is made for any guest out of 200, the number generally in the house, Willard, without a moment's hesitation, and without ever referring to the book, can tell when he arrived and the number of his room.

We found the streets of New York covered with frozen snow, in some places three and four feet deep. The weather is intensely cold, in fact I never knew before what cold was and as I have not altered my usual clothing, I feel it " pretty considerable sharp."

New York is the Island of Manhattan, on a point of land at the confluence of the East River, and the Hudson as far as

memory goes. There is not much worth seeing except the view
of the bay from the Battery. In Summer it must be a very
beautiful prospect, but at present everything looks bleak and
cold.

New York has few architectural beauties to attract the
traveller. Yet it is worthy of a visit, and is a place of interest
as the great commercial mart on the Eastern coast of a country,
which gives fair promise of being the most powerful and
prosperous nation that ever was founded.

18th. On the morning of the 18th we left for Philadelphia,
went by steam boat to Amboy, by railroad from thence to the
Delaware, and across that river to Philadelphia. This journey,
of about 100 miles, we performed in nine hours, for three
dollars.

On board the steamer there was a raw heterogeneous
assemblage of several hundred people so closely stowed together
that we had scarcely room to stand. There might be seen the
slaveholder from the South, the abolitionist from the North, the
merchant, the Congress man, the lawyer, the artizan, and
labourer, all huddled together in glorious equality, smelling of
anti fogmatics, and in the most independent manner, spitting
and smoking almost in each other's faces. Dollars and cents were
the burthen of the conversation. At the end of the cabin was a
bar at which the favourite beverages, gin and cocktail, were
supplied to the thirsty souls. From what I have seen, I should
think that temperance societies are very much required. They
all seem to be inebriate dram drinkers, what with their bitters
in the morning, their gin sling, and brandy and water during
the day. They are continually boozing from the hour they rise
till they go to bed. Morning, noon and night, it is all the
same, and it is stupefying, brutalizing, solitary sottishness they
indulge in, not from any conviviality of feeling or love of good
fellowship but from pure, downright sottishness. This was the
first American steamer I was aboard of, and I must confess, I

was not altogether in love with it, but this, I suppose is the effect of prejudice.

Amboy is a small village, consisting of a few scattered houses, on a pretty bay of the River Raritan. The drive from this to the Delaware is through a flat uninteresting country, the sandy plains of Jersey. A great part of the country is covered with stunted pines, and in some places, cedar and maple swamps.

On our arrival at Philadelphia, tried at several hotels before we could get rooms. At last succeeded at the American Hotel kept by Captain Saint. Mr. R., our fellow voyager across the Atlantic, was very attentive shewing us the sights, and introducing us to his acquaintances. We should have found Philadelphia very dull without his assistance. We had a letter of introduction to Mr. Brown, but all the notice the old curmudgeon took of it, was to leave his card.

Mr. R. introduced us to a very fine old gentleman, Mr. Vaughan of The American Philosophical Society. We breakfasted with him one morning when he shewed us the curiosities of the institution, amongst others, a very interesting document, the original of the Declaration of Independence, in the handwriting of Jefferson. Was at a *conversazione* one night. A large party of gentlemen met ostensibly for literary and scientific conversation, but the serious business of the evening was eating stewed oysters, and drinking punch.

The situation of Philadelphia is very good and evokes both the taste and judgment of "Friend Penn." It rests between the rivers Delaware and Schuylkill, the latter in the Indian language, signifies " the hidden stream," so called, I suppose, from the luxuriant forests that overhung its banks. Population 200,000; streets all run at right angles, clean and neat; the houses well built and comfortable looking, with a certain uniformity and quakerishness of appearance. There are some very fine public buildings, constructed with fine white marble. The market is very extensive and well arranged, and the waterworks which supply the town, from the simplicity and ingenuity of their construction, are well worth a visit.

After Church on Sunday, went to a Quaker meeting. The congregation sat in solemn silence for an hour, and then separated without a word being spoken. They were the most ridiculously grave-looking gentlemen I ever saw. Had great difficulty in keeping my countenance. Henry, at last, fell fast asleep, snoring most obstreperously and wakened with a loud snort, just as the congregation rose to depart. It was too ridiculous. We had scarcely got to the door when we burst out laughing, greatly to the consternation of the Broad Brims, who rebuked us by their looks. Verily, verily, we behaved in a very unseemly manner. We then went to the Catholic Cathedral where there was the very reverse of simplicity.

On the journey from New York to Philadelphia we passed close to the residence of Joseph Buonaparte near Bordentown, 30 miles from Philadelphia. There the Monarch of two kingdoms and the brother of him who once swayed the destinies of Europe, leads the life of a quiet country gentleman, the situation for which, I think, Nature designed him. He is much respected, and esteemed by his neighbours, and bears the character of a kind hearted, amiable man.

26th. Left for Baltimore—Sailed some distance up the Delaware, then by railroad across to the Chesapeak, and from thence by steam-boat to Baltimore.

The Chesapeak is a very fine sheet of water, the Susquehanna, the Elk, the Rappahannock, the Potomac, Patapsco, the James River, and several others flow into it. Little more than two centuries ago, no barque larger than the light canoe of the Indian had navigated its waters. Its banks were clothed with the ancient forest, through whose depths a white man had never penetrated; and now, the ships of many nations convey over its waves, the products of other lands. The old woods have been felled, the thicket and the swamp have yielded to the cultivated farm and roads and railways, crowded with travellers, hurrying along in the eager pursuit of gain, intersect the hunting grounds where the free Indian once roamed. The red men have been swept gradually Westward by the rushing tide of civilization. Most of them are now on the other side of the Mississippi, and of the few tribes who yet remained to the Eastward of that river, some are preparing to cross it according to treaties with the United States, while some are struggling desperately to retain possession of the country where the bones of their fathers are buried.

Baltimore is by far the prettiest situated town I have yet seen in America. The approach to it by water affords, I think, the best view. A creek of the river Patapsco runs a considerable way into the land, forming a secure land-locked harbour. Round the extremity of this, the town is built with elevated land at each side, and in the background a range of wooded hills.

Col. Moore, extremely kind, has introduced us to all his friends, parties and invitations without number.

The Americans might be described as a handshaking generation. Whenever a gentleman is introduced, he seizes your hand and gives it about half a dozen hearty shakes. I have put a great many people through my hands since I arrived, but I don't like this indiscriminate hand-shaking. It is an operation I would rather decline.

Received an invitation to go to Winchester in Virginia to witness the ceremony of opening a railroad, which has been constructed from that place to Harper's Ferry. The party consisted of the Directors, President, Col. Moore and some other guests. Stopped at Harper's Ferry the first evening. The drive to that is very beautiful. The road runs along the Patapsco where high and craggy banks are covered with lofty trees, and a thick underwood of short-leaved laurel. The scenery at Harper's Ferry is very grand. Jefferson, in his notes on Virginia, says it is worth while to cross the Atlantic to visit it. I have seen bolder and more sublime scenery, and scenery of more exquisite loveliness in our own country, but still it is inexpressibly beautiful. The rivers Potomac and Shenandoah meeting here, burst their way through a barrier of rock, precipitous cliffs crowned with dark pine wood frown over the river on each side, and form the pass to the lovely Valley of the Shenandoah, which is one of the finest districts in Virginia. This valley extends nearly 200 miles, bounded on one side by a lofty range of wooded mountains called the Blue Ridge, and on the other by the Alleghanies.

The view from the top of the rock on either side of Harper's Ferry is indeed glorious, but there is scarcely a pleasure in this world without an alloy of pain. No blessing without a curse close upon it, and this scenery is subject to the general rule. There is a most abominable little village just in the pass between the mountains. Here is the Government Manufactory of Firearms, and the smell of coal smoke, and the clanking of hammers obtrude themselves on the senses and prevent your enjoyment from being unmixed. What induced the Government to establish a manufactory at such an out-of-the-way place, I cannot imagine, unless because it *was* out-of-the-way, and therefore safe from an invading enemy.

On our arrival at Winchester, received with a salute of artillery, and all the musical instruments of every description in the town struck up a deafening din to do honour to the party. We formed a procession, and marched two and two to the tune of Yankee Doodle to a large building, where a platform was erected on which we, that is to say, the members of the deputation and the guests, took our seats. The house was soon filled, and a gentleman rose and made a long " noration " on the occasion, in which he talked much of ancient Rome and Palmyra, Oliver Cromwell and General Washington, steam engines and the Cholera Morbus. He compared the ladies present to the lillies of the valley, at which they blushed and giggled, and he concluded by proving, evidently to the satisfaction of the meeting, that there was no country like America, and that the American people were the bravest, noblest, and most intelligent on the face of the globe.

There was a large dinner party in the evening at which they did us the honour to drink our health.

Next morning Col. Moore left us on his return to Baltimore, we remained for another public dinner to which we were invited. Met a countryman, a Captain Glassock of the British service, his regiment quartered at Quebec. He was on leave of absence, and had been staying for some time with a friend in Virginia. He seemed to be on the most intimate terms with every one and, as far as I could judge, a great favourite. We got horses and set out together to take a ride. He said he would introduce us at some houses in the neighbourhood.

In the course of the ride, he very unreservedly told us his history, the sum of which was, that when he was a poor boy Ensign, and when little more than eighteen years old, he fell desperately in love, married, and at forty years of age found himself a widower with a captain's commission and two daughters. I never saw a person better calculated to get comfortably on through the world no matter in what circumstances he might be placed. He was a tall, very athletic person, with a rollicking air and his jolly good-humoured face, like that of brave Captn. Magan :

" As broad as a big frying pan,"

was of a very rubicund complexion, which I, in the innocence of my heart, believed to be caused by an inordinate attachment to the brandy bottle. But he assured me that it was entirely owing to his temperate habits, " for," said he, " here am I, who have been kicked about for the last twenty years in every clime. I have been frozen in Canada, and broiled in the East Indies and, thank Heaven, owing to my strict temperance, I still retain my decent Irish complexion, not like the yellow snakes of fellows you see in this country. Now, my dear Sir," said he, " you are going to travel here, and I would just take the liberty of hinting to you that there is no getting on comfortably in this country without an abundance of soft language, always have a civil expression on your tongue, and you will find the Virginians at least, an accommodating sort of people. You may perceive how often I use the word ' Sir,' no matter whom I address. I shall be ridiculed and laughed at, when I return to my regiment, but I know the value of civil language. It is a coin that passes current everywhere, and you spend it liberally without lightening your purse." The captain acted up to his doctrine. He had a civil word for everyone, and whenever he had occasion to ask for anything, he always did it in the blandest manner, and with the mcst insinuating tone of voice.

We called at several houses and, as a matter of course, were asked to remain for dinner. The Virginians are a hospitable, generous people. Virginia was colonized principally by Cavaliers. The inhabitants are proud of their origin and are fond of calling their state the " old dominion."

April 1836

On our way to Baltimore, stopped at a little place called Charlestown, where we met considerable attention. Were at two parties. Have received several more invitations, in fact we could scarcely get away. Spent the evening with a Dr. Yates, who had a party of young ladies to meet us, and a very merry party we had. Next day, dined with Dr. Cramer, a worthy, warm-hearted, Irishman; he pressed us to stay some time. On taking leave of him, he gave me his blessing and his walking stick, which he begged me to keep in memory of him.

On our return to Baltimore, were very gay, at parties every night. Found very pleasant acquaintances in the family of Mrs. Armistead, sister of Mr. Moore, and widow of Colonel Armistead, who successfully defended Fort McHenry against the English in 1814.

7th April. Left Baltimore at nine o'clock in the morning by railroad. Arrived in Washington at twelve o'clock, went to the Capitol, to the Senate, saw Judge Porter, to whom we had a letter of introduction from Mr. Sampson, also Mr. G. Lee and Mr. W. Kerr, Members of Congress, to whom Colonel Moore had given us letters. The judge received us very kindly like a good Irishman, as he is, and engaged us to dine with him on Saturday.

8th. My thoughts are still wandering back to the lovely valley of the Shenandoah. I should like to revisit it in Autumn, but I fear that cannot be. I forgot to mention a visit we paid to a fine old gentleman, who lived in a most delightful spot, a quiet nook, retired from the hurry and bustle of the world. The house was built on a green knoll. A few venerable trees overshadowed it. Along the front of the building extended a verandah — then as we rode up, we found the old gentleman slowly pacing about enjoying the warmth of a sweet Spring evening. We gave our horses in charge to some black children, who were rolling about, and basking in the sun, and preceded by our friend the captain, went up to pay our respects to Mr. Lee. He was a very gentlemanlike man. He had been educated in one of the English universities, had travelled through Europe and had the polish and information of a man who had seen the world, and mixed in the best society. I felt particular interest in meeting him, as he had been the relative and intimate friend of Washington.

The view from his house, look what way you would, presented such a combination of forest and waters, wooded hills, and sloping lawns, as formed a most charming landscape.

I was never in a country where noble parks and beautiful demesnes, could be so easily, so quickly, and at so little expense, formed. The material is there — all that is necessary is a judicious disposition of it, but the Americans have no taste for such things. In a country where the landed property of a country is not kept together, but is continually undergoing divisions and subdivisions, there is little inducement to raise such homes as are found in England.

Whatever evils may arise from a law of primogeniture, it has at least this advantage, it tends much to beautify and improve a country. A man naturally feels a strong affection for his hereditary home, with which are connected the most tender and endearing recollections of his life. It is with no common interest that he views the scenes of his own and his offspring's childhood, and he feels a just pride in keeping up the old homestead and transmitting it unimpaired to his heir. He knows that his work is not in vain, that he has an interest in it beyond his own life. To this feeling are owing the stately halls of England with their noble parks and woods — the fine old manor houses, the comfortable dwellings of the substantial yeomen and their well tended farms, which stud the face of the country, and give such a charming aspect of cultivated beauty, as cannot be surpassed in the wide world. But in America, where property is subject to constant subdivision and sale, a man has no inducement to build and to plant. His property to him is just worth what it will sell for, it has no extrinsic value. He cares no more for it than for any other property of equal value — he sells it without a pang. He has no home feeling, no local attachments, and this appears to me a very unamiable trait in the American character.

Washington is situated in the district of Columbia, composed of a territory ten miles square, ceded by the States of Virginia and Maryland, and under the government of the *United States*.

Washington is the mere skeleton of a city. The original place which is very extensive, will never, I think be filled up. The most that can be said for it is that it will be a very fine city when it is built. The principal street called Pennsylvania Avenue is very spacious, and about a mile long, but there are no good houses in it. At one extremity on a slight eminence, is the President's official residence, a handsome building of white marble. At the other extremity, also on an eminence, stands the Capitol, which is certainly a noble structure, but in my opinion rather deformed by the huge, broad dome that over-hangs it in front, there is an imposing portico supported on Corinthian marble pillars. Over one side of the grand entrance is a magnificent statue of Mars, and on the other one of Smiling Peace, bearing on her hand the olive branch. They were executed, I believe, by an Italian artist.

You first enter a large circular Hall, lighted from above by the Dome. Round the Hall, in different compartments, are several large paintings representing "The Declaration of American Independence, 1776," "General Washington resigning his commission of Commander-in-Chief, 1783," and, the "Surrender of General Burgoyne and Lord Cornwallis."

From the Rotunda, doors open on the passages leading to the Senate and House of Representatives, and the different offices connected with them. The Senate Chamber is a handsome semi-circular apartment surrounded by a Gallery, to which the public have free access, and which is generally crowded with visitors, among whom are always a considerable number of ladies.

The House of Representatives is a very fine room, built on the same place as the Senate Chamber, but much more spacious. Each member is provided with a desk, and a *spitting box*. By-the-bye, I think if the desks were removed, it would have the effect of shortening Hon. Members' speeches very much, for I observe they generally have a heap of notes to refer to, and with the aid of a bundle of manuscripts, they can spin out their speeches to a most unconscionable length.

Last week, a long-winded fellow spoke for three days, resuming his speech each morning after it had been adjourned from the preceding evening. I must say that the business of the nation is conducted with great decorum and propriety, far more so than in our House of Commons. I never heard any expressions either of assent or disapprobation and no attempt at coughing down an unpopular speaker, though it must be a precious privilege to be enabled to put a stopper on a prosy speaker. It is too bad that the time and patience of several hundred people should be consumed in enduring the twaddle of some fellow afflicted with a *"cacoethes loquendi."*

9th. Mr. McKim had his carriage waiting for us at ten o'clock to take us to the President's. On our arrival there, we were shewn into an ante-room. After waiting a minute, the servant returned and ushered us into the Den of the old Lion. I had a great curiosity to see him, from the accounts I had heard, I pictured to myself a rough, tough, old Hickory sort of person, and was surprised to find him possessed of such urbanity of manner. He received us with great courtesy, shook hands with us, begged us to be seated, and at once entered into conversation on the usual topics. He soon began talking of the French Question. I told him how strongly public opinion in England was in favour of America on that question, and how all parties had agreed in condemning the conduct of the French Government, as shuffling and dishonourable, and in approving the spirited conduct of the President in maintaining the dignity of the U.S. The old General seemed much pleased.

He talked of the bank question, abused the banking system, said he never wished to see a bank in the country. He disapproved of railroad companies as creating monopolies, " and monopolies," said he, "in every shape and form I will oppose; they tend to aristocracy, and that," continued he, putting his heel emphatically against the floor, " I will strenuously resist." I was surprised to hear him talk so unreservedly as he did of the conduct of General Gaines, who is engaged against the Seminole Indians. He condemned it warmly, pointed out where he was wrong, said how he should have acted, and declared had he been there he would have terminated the war in a few days. After some further conversation we rose to take our leave. He again shook hands with us, wished us a pleasant tour, and bade us good-morning, and so ended our interview with " Old Hickory."

In person he is very tall, his frame is gaunt and emaciated, his face is long, pale and wrinkled, his hair is nearly white, thick and shaggy, and combed back off his forehead. Altogether he is a remarkable looking person and a man of very uncommon character. His whole life has been a constant scene of violence and excitement, hardship and toil and danger were, for long time, familiars to him. Possessed of undaunted courage and uncontrollable energy he has succeeded in cases where more calculating men would have failed. He keeps on his way with unyielding firmness of purpose, and beats down and passes over everything that opposes him. If an obstacle is in his path, no matter of what nature, he overcomes it, his passions are violent, his friendships and enmities are both extreme.

He hates everything that stands in his way, he will hate an abstract proposition with as much intensity and bitterness as he would a personal or political opponent. His bursts of passion are said to be sometimes terrible. He will lash himself into a rage, leap up, storm and swear like a Hector; yet, it is said, on occasions, his passion fits are well timed and intended. He possesses great sagacity and knowledge of human nature, and can very adroitly avail himself of the prejudices and passions of others. His services in the field have been great. It is perhaps to his military exploits that he owes his great popularity with the mass of the people.

When a boy, he served in the Revolutionary War. In the next war, he saved New Orleans, under every disadvantage, with undisciplined men, without anyone in whom he could repose confidence. He had none to rely on but himself; his activity was wonderful; he compelled everyone to serve, took all responsibility on himself; inspired all with his own dauntless energy, and won the day.

He is amazingly popular with the mass of the people, unpopular, generally with the men of wealth and standing who fear that his measures may lead to uncontrollable democracy. But almost all parties give him credit for honesty of purpose.

From the President's we drove to the house of the Vice-President, and found him at home. We sat for some time with him. The principal conversation was about the Seminole Indians. Martin Van Buren is a very sharp-looking little gentleman. He has a very intellectual forehead, keen little grey eyes, foxy-coloured whiskers, hair grey, and worn long behind. He is esteemed so clever as to have acquired the name of " the Magician," and from the utter repugnance he has ever shewn to give a direct answer to any question, or to declare openly and explicitly his sentiments on any one point, he has been favoured with the appellation of the " non-committal " man. One thing alone is known with every certainty as to his real feelings, and that is, he is most firmly and conscientiously attached to himself, and pursues with most unvarying devotion his own interests. No matter how much he may double and turn, they are the objects of which he is always in pursuit.

The same day, Judge Porter drove us out into the country to pay a visit to the widow of Theobald W. Tone. She is a very fine old lady, with wonderful vivacity, and still retains a strong touch of the brogue both on the tongue and heart — her feelings are enthusiastically Irish.

Spent a very pleasant evening with Judge Porter, in company with a small party of clever men. We had H. Clay, the most distinguished man in America. Mr. K., the other Senator from Kentucky, also a very able man, a fine frank open hearted Kentuckian, a diamond, but an unpolished one. There was also Professor Palfrey of Boston, shrewd, acute and remarkably well-informed, a good specimen of a Yankee *gentleman*.

11th. Drove to Mount Vernon, a lovely spot, but sadly neglected. It might be made a paradise on earth. The drive to it, for a considerable distance, lies through woodlands, where the traveller may choose whatever route he chooses. Regular road there is none, not even an avenue near the house, unless a track like the rough bed of a mountain stream can be called so. The place appears to have been allowed to go wild, untouched by the hand of man since the death of its illustrious proprietor. The house (a wooden one) was erected by Washington on a site admirably selected. It is built on a green eminence, embosomed in woods and commanding a view of the lovely Potomac, whose wooded banks, appearing to meet in the distance, give to the river the appearance of a lake. Along the side of the house, facing the river, runs an open piazza. A lawn slopes down a short way to where the bank becomes steep and wooded.

Mrs. W., a grand niece of the General, resides here now. We
sent in our cards and obtained permission to see the house.
There was an air of extreme melancholy and loneliness in the
deserted appearance of the garden. The gate old and rickety
was creaking in every blast. The box borders, totally neglected,
had grown up into bushes. Weeds were on the walks, part of
the conservatory was in ruins. It had been burnt down and
never restored. The other part was crammed full of lemon and
orange trees, badly attended to; altogether it was "the abomination of desolation."

In a little dell near the house, in the shade of some cedar
trees, is the grave of Washington. It is a simple vault surrounded by a brick wall. Over the gate is the inscription
" Within this enclosure rest the remains of General George
Washington." As I stood there, I felt it is one of the holiest
spots of earth, which contains the bones of him who had conferred such benefits on mankind. Freedom's own blessed and
glorious champion, the Father of his country, the incorruptible
Patriot, the pure statesman, the Good man. While the fame of
kings and warriors, whose selfish ambition has devastated the
earth and filled it with tears and blood, must fade in time,
George Washington's glory will never die, for it is founded on
a basis that is immortal. Never did man earn for himself a
prouder name or acquire more true and genuine glory. He
drew his sword in the holiest cause in which man can be
engaged. He battled for the right, and was so highly favoured
as to see his efforts crowned with success, and his country
fairly started on the path of national prosperity and happiness.

Judge Porter has been very attentive to us. We have spent
another pleasant evening with Mr. Clay and Mr. Crittenden.

Hearing that the Government was about to send an
expedition towards the Rocky Mountains, I thought it would
be a good opportunity to visit that country. The Judge introduced me to the Adjutant General, as the person able to give

me every information. He kindly offered me a letter to the commanding officer and said, if I wished to go, he would take care that every facility and assistance should be afforded to me, but as the party will be away four months at least, I cannot spare the time, so we have determined on going to the South.

There is a war at present, being carried on in Florida against the Seminole Indians. It has long been evident that the Red and White man cannot live in societies close to each other without great peril to both, and without injury and degradation to the former in particular. The Indian will not assimilate himself to the habits of the Whites. He looks with utter scorn and contempt on the arts of civilized life. He considers the Whites slaves, and he distrusts them as enemies. His path, and that of the " pale faces," lie not in the same track. He is a warrior and a hunter, a free roamer of the woods and the prairies. The Government of the U.S. thought there was a necessity for removing the Indians farther back. Accordingly they determined to assign lands (very kind, is it not to give lands to which the Indians have a better right than themselves?) on the West of the Mississippi, to such of the tribes as still remain to the East of that river. The Seminoles, however, were not convinced of the justice of this, and were determined to resist. War took place.

The Indians commenced operations by attacking a detachment of troops consisting of upwards of a hundred men, and scalping every man with the exception of one, who contrived to make his escape. What is extraordinary, the dead bodies which were found about a month afterwards by General Gaines' army, were not plundered of the slightest article except their arms, as if the Indians wished to show that it was no common motive which incited them to war.

Shola, their chief, is said to be a very clever man. He has certainly shown a great deal of able conduct in this war. He led Gaines into a position where he and his whole army must have surrendered, or been scalped in two days, if it had not been for the opportune arrival of General Clinch with a reinforcement.

It is said to be impossible to change permanently the habits of an Indian, the attempt has been made. There are several instances of Indian boys having been sent to colleges, there receiving a good education and mixing for years in society, and on their return to their tribe, flinging off the garb of civilization, and betaking themselves with joy to the forests, preferring the wild liberty of a hunter's life, to the conventional restraints of society.

News today from Texas. The Fort of San Antonio taken by Santa Anna, and all the garrison put to the sword. Among those who fell, was that curious character Col. Crockett. A short time ago he was candidate for the representation of some District in Congress. The speech he made to the electors on that occasion was very characteristic of the man, short, but not *sweet*. He said, " If you elect me I shall endeavour to discharge my duty faithfully, if you do not, you may go to Hell, and I'll go to Texas." To Texas he went, and got knocked on the head.

This war in Texas is altogether a most infamous affair. It has been got up principally by land jobbers in the U.S. who do not scruple to deluge that province with blood in order to indulge in their speculating propensities.

How much do actions, which, when viewed at a distance, appear glorious and brilliant, lose their brightness when we look closer into them, and know the persons who achieved them and the motives by which they were influenced. The knowledge of how much transactions which occur in our own times are misrepresented and falsely glossed over, is sufficient to give us a painful distrust of history, and to shake our belief in those bright passages which at long intervals relieve the dark record of human crime and misery.

The Texans, whose fame has been trumpeted forth as the heroic champions of liberty, and for whom the sympathies of freemen are so loudly claimed: what are they, but a band composed of the very scum and sweepings of the United States, refugees from justice, unprincipled adventurers, outcasts from society, and restless spirits who cannot brook the restraints of civilized life and the control of laws. Such are the men who rally round the standard of revolt in Texas. And the vaunted heroism that was displayed at San Antonio—what was it but the brute knavery of desperate ruffians?

Returned to Baltimore.

Henry Tyler and I spent a morning practising with one of the best rifle shots of this part of the country. Made almost as good shooting as he did.

19th. The hour after midnight. Just returned from a very gay ball at a private house. Let us revisit it and I will introduce you to an American ballroom: how crowded are the rooms, and what a number of pretty women there are; few distinguished beauties, but many, very many faces that one loves to look at. The ladies are well dressed too. So are the gentlemen and there is nothing in their appearance, or manner, by which you could distinguish them from a company in an English ballroom. The only thing that strikes you as strange is, that the musicians are coloured people—and I may add, that you will scarcely hear any gentleman present addressed by a title lower than that of field officer at least.

Let us take our stand here, and I will point out some of the people to you: that pretty animated little girl with fair hair, fresh complexion, and merry blue eyes that twinkle brightly through the long dark lashes, is Miss E. M. She is, I believe, an only daughter, does what she pleases in her papa's house and gives very pleasant parties. Her voice is like a singing bird's, how musical is her laugh with its clear silvery tones ringing from the pure metal of the heart. That lady seated at the end of the room, figure *en bon point* dressed in a robe of rich black velvet, and wearing a profusion of jewels, was the wife of a King, Jerome Buonaparte. She was, I am told, eminently handsome, and she still does retain the traces of former beauty. The young lady to whom she is speaking is her niece Miss P., one of the belles of Baltimore.

Remark that tall slight lady in the centre of the room, now she turns her head, what a glorious face, glowing with youth and joy and intelligence. What expression! Every feature speaks. Did you ever see a more finely formed head, a more serene and noble brow? They are such as Phidias would have loved to copy, and her mouth now slightly parted in a smile, how inexpressibly beautiful it is? Altogether it is one of the faces of such surpassing loveliness which one seldom sees, but in a dream. But, but, alas, her figure is wretched, long, thin and gawky, her motions are ungraceful. Her step is heavy, uncertain without the slightest ease or elasticity. She has the face of a goddess, but the figure of a Yankee. A majority of the ladies have good eyes and delicate complexions.

That low, slight made effeminate-looking young man dressed with scrupulous exactness, gold chains round his neck, and rings on his delicate fingers, enough to make the stock-in-trade of a dozen pedlars, is the most consummate fop, and conceited coxcomb I had ever the fortune to meet. He has scarcely spoken a word since he entered the room. Of course he does not dance, as he declares the very thought of being pushed about so horrifies him, and the quick motions of the dancers makes him frightfully nervous. There he has been standing all evening with his *chapeau bras* in one hand and a curious looking walking stick in the other. He is rich, has been in Europe, travelled there a short time, and returned with his head turned, and it seems inflated with the ambition of being the Beau Brummell of America.

Let us look into this little room, what a merry knot of elderly gentlemen. That comfortable-looking, fattish person with a pleasant twinkle in his eye, and a half drained champagne glass in his hand is Professor D., who, with his puns and witticisms is keeping them all in a roar. The little gentleman who is laughing in that peculiar cackling note, with which a hen proclaims her safe delivery, is Col. T., and that tall portly good-looking gentleman is my worthy, and esteemed friend Col. M. But enough of this; it is time to go to bed.

Engaged our passage to Charleston in the Brig Genl. Marion, Capt. Delano.

Friday 22nd. Dined with Col. Moore in company with the Misses Armistead: spent as we thought our last evening together and bade farewell, supposing we were to sail that night at twelve o'clock. Went on board and found the vessel would not start till morning. Rose early next day—went on board and told by the Captain we should not sail till Sunday morning. Another day's repose. That evening met Mr. Crawford, just returned from his tour in the South, spent the last night together at Mrs. Armistead's.

Sunday 24th. Sailed at sunrise, beautiful day, but so calm, we have made little way.

25th. Another fine day, as the wind was ahead, and no chance of getting out of the bay. Came to an anchor in Hampton Road. Henry, the Captain, another passenger and I, took the boat and went on shore. Had some rifle shooting in the thick pine woods, which cover this part of the country.

Glorious sunset. I have seldom seen such a one. No pencil could copy, no pen could describe the beauty of the scene. The sun slowly sank behind a broken bank of vermillion coloured clouds, throwing across the smooth bay, a broad shining track of golden light, which gradually fading, as he disappeared, was succeeded for a few moments by a rosy flush that made the waters glow. The parting smile of the day god before he retired to his rest.

" The sun set, and up rose the yellow moon."

And the stars, the bright-eyed, mysterious stars that keep their watch in Heaven, the sparkling orbs that gem the infinity of space, whom the fond superstition of an earlier age regarded as exercising a peculiar influence over man's destiny—they are wheeling round their blazing axles, and, while performing their allotted courses, they give light and joy to other systems. Away in the far blue ether they shed their gentle and subdued beams on our globe. No wonder that the earlier inhabitants of the world bowed down in adoration before the bright host of Heaven.

What a delicious night, the vessel is riding at anchor, silent and motionless. At half a mile's distance lies the long, low, wooded coast, from whose dark pine groves are occasionally heard the mournful notes of the Whip-poor-Will. The dark blue Heaven above me (and it may be fancy, but I think I never saw the sky so intensely blue, nor the stars so bright) and the smooth moonlit waters around me, combined with the deep silence, powerfully affect the mind. The calm beauty of the scene sinks into the heart with a softening influence, and lifts the thoughts to aspirations, and wishes that are not of this world. In such a scene, at such an hour, the harsh and gloomy passions of our nature are subdued and chastened, even as the rugged outlines of the scenery are mellowed and beautified by the beams of the moon. And then the heart loves to indulge either in reminiscences of the past, or under the influence of that longing which nothing on earth can satisfy, rises to the contemplation of that dim coast beyond the tomb to which the dark stream of time is so rapidly sweeping us.

Bright lamps of Heaven, ye may soon be shining on my grave, be it so.

26th. Morning is on the waters, bright and joyous, we have every sail set and under the impetus of a fresh breeze the little brig is bounding merrily over the waves.

Henry is standing at the bows, popping away at every bird that comes within range of his rifle. The old skipper, a curious specimen of the species, by the way, is sitting with his coat off in his favourite position on the deck, his back leaning against the taffrail, and his knees drawn close up to his chin. And our friend, the Georgian, and a female passenger, are below, practising a duet of puking. They are "cruel bad."

The woman with an infant at her breast, is on her way to look for her husband, who is somewhere in Florida, and the *gentleman* from Georgia, is on his way home. He is a " brute baste," and is continually hawking, spitting, and belching, and practising all manner of abomination.

The little brig is deeply laden with whiskey, flour and bacon, so there is no fear of starvation. Our accommodation is none of the best, but I am quite reconciled to it. It is much pleasanter to be at sea this weather, or indeed any weather, than to be jolted over most abominable roads, through an uninteresting country like North Carolina, in one of those outlandish vehicles, an American stage coach. Our cabin is small and so low that I cannot stand upright. My berth is about four feet and a half long. It requires some ingenuity to coil myself up in it and, moreover, it is the nest of a numerous progeny of bugs, who, scruple not to take the most unwarrantable liberties with my person.

The man who officiates as cook and steward is a Malay. He is rather a picturesque-looking object with his bronzed face, glittering eyes, and long shining black hair tied behind and hanging over his shoulders, like a horse's tail. When he attends at dinner, by way of making himself look smart, he wears his shirt sleeves tucked up to his shoulders.

It is said " God sends meat, and the Devil sends cooks." In

this instance I think his Imperial Majesty has had the com-
plaisance to send one of the artists from his own kitchen —
garlic, tallow and treacle are the favourite ingredients of every
dish. Today we had a great treat, in the shape of a nondescript
pudding, which Mr. Cook set on the table with a flourish, and
a look of conscious merit, as if he considered it a master stroke
of his genius.

28th. Last two days we have been standing off and on,
unable to double Cape Hatteras. This is a very dangerous point,
the scene of many a shipwreck. Shoals run out from the shore
20 or 30 miles, rendering the navigation very perilous. The only
inhabitant of this bleak and desolate coast, is an old fellow
called Mitchelt, who has lived for many years here, practising
the profitable profession of land pirate. In the winter months
the shore is strewed with wrecks, and then he reaps a rich
harvest. When the ship is in the breakers, and the shriek of the
drowning mariner is heard in the pauses of the storm, then the
old gentleman is in motion " as busy as the Devil in a gale
of wind " — and picks up many a prize.

The skipper has been telling me stories about him, and his
domicile, his house, built of the timbers of wrecks, and ornamented on the inside with the figure heads of many goodly
ships, is well stored with the luxuries of foreign lands. The old
boy dresses in a peculiar style, wears his beard to his girdle.
He has no neighbours to quarrel with. He rules in undisturbed
supremacy, has plenty of game of all sorts for the shooting,
and lives like a prince " taking the good the gods provide him."

As there is little prospect at present of getting out of this
position, I wanted the Captain to put us ashore in the boat, that
we might pay our respects to this old man of the sea; but he
assures me that such a tremendous surf rolls in on the beach,
that no boat could land.

It is very warm, the pitch in the seams of the deck is boiling in the heat. Several sharks have been prowling about the vessel today, seeking what they might devour.

29th. Another bright calm day, there is scarcely a breath of wind. The sails are flapping dully against the mast, and the Captain has nearly blown all the breath out of his body whistling for a breeze that will not come. Away on the verge of the horizon, the low coast is barely visible, appearing over the water like the dark ridge of a wave. This the place to enjoy the luxury of laziness. The vessel is heaving gently on the smooth and glittering sea, whose surface is at times disturbed by the sparkling gambols of some frolicksome porpoise. The sailors are loitering idly on deck, and I am sitting on the bow-sprit watching some vessels that are a few miles distant, and wondering when we shall get round this eternal Cape Hatteras.

A storm would be preferable to this dull, dead calm. The thermometer stands at ninety — pretty warm I guess.

30th. A breeze sprung up last night, which enabled us to weather Cape Hatteras at last, and we are now standing to at the rate of eight knots an hour. Glorious day, steady wind, the sea is roughened, and sparkling flying fish are darting about in every direction. Occasionally a turtle rises to the surface a moment to breathe, and then disappears. Porpoises are gambling round the bows, and at times that ravenous monster of the deep, the great Atlantic shark, appears near the vessel, his dorsal fin showing above the water, as he slowly cruises along.

The Captain has rigged out a fishing line. Caught two Alba-cors — beautiful fish, back purple, green and gold; sides like polished silver. On such a day as this, with a fresh breeze, the bright sky over our heads, the sparkling sea around us and the creatures of the deep sporting on its surface, one feels the heart beat freer, the blood courses more fleetly through the veins and life is felt to be a blessing.

May 1836

1st May. Becalmed.

2nd May. Dead calm; smooth sea; blazing sun; the pitch boiling out of the seams of the deck. Caught a lot of fish today as many as will feast the whole ship's company for days.

4th. Arrived at Charleston this evening, having been eleven days performing a run of 600 miles.

Tried four or five hotels and found them all full. At last succeeded in getting a double-bedded room about the dimensions of a rat-trap, and glad to get even into such a hole.

Charleston, the chief town of South Carolina, is seated on a narrow strip of land between the Ashley and Cooper Rivers. For an American town it is rather old-looking. The majority of the houses are wooden, painted white, with a piazza extending along the front. This, in a warm climate, is almost necessary, and at Charleston in summer, it is hot enough, in all conscience.

The streets are lined with rows of a pretty tree called " the Pride of India." The flowers, something like the lilac, perfume the air, and the fresh green of the leaves relieves the glare of the white walls and gives an air of coolness to the streets.

A stranger here is struck with the number, and tameness, of the Turkey Buzzard. These disgusting birds are of the vulture tribe, and they may be constantly seen hovering over the streets, sitting on the housetops, and walking above the market, looking out for grub. They pick up all the offal and filth of the town, they are blessed with good appetites and sometimes stuff themselves so full that they are obliged to disgorge. This operation they often perform as they are flying over the streets, and woe be to the unfortunate wight on whom their favours descend—the waters of the Atlantic could not wash the marks

of the abomination from his clothes—the perfumes of Araby
could not conquer the insufferable odour. These birds are found
so useful that they are protected by the civic authorities. There
is a fine of five dollars inflicted for killing one.

The society here, I have been told, is very pleasant, but at
this season all persons able to leave the place migrate to the
North. The neighbourhood is flat and swampy, well suited for
the production of rice, but not favourable to human life. In
Summer they are visited by yellow fever, and another disease
as deadly called the Country Fever. It is said to be certain death
to spend a night now in the country, or the vicinity, of the rice
plantations.

There is nothing of any interest to be seen in Charleston.
Indeed, throughout America there are few classic spots, few
places whose historical recollections would induce you to visit
them. Here are no venerable cathedrals in whose shrines are
entombed the remains of kings and warriors, no lofty pillared
aisles, none of those ruined castles whose very antiquity hal-
lows them and whose time worn battlements, and ivy-coloured
walls, awaken in the mind of the most careless observer,
thoughts of the deeds of other years—here are no relics of
feudal power—here are no *ruins*—everything in this land is in
the vigor and spring of youth.

But there are places on which Americans may look with
just pride. They may point with triumph to the site of those
battlefields where undisciplined peasants fought the good fight
of liberty and elevated their country from the degraded state
of a province to the dignity of an independent nation. They
may point to what their enterprise and industry have achieved,
their rail roads, their canals, their harbours, the smiling corn-
fields, which, but a few years ago, were dense forests tenanted
by the wolf and the savage. They may point to their un-
exampled prosperity, their flourishing manufactures, their
extensive commerce, their overflowing treasury. They may

enumerate all they have done, and in that find the best answer to those who cavil at their political institutions.

It cannot be denied that the U.S. Government has effected to an eminent degree, the end of all right government, the good of the people. The political problem, whether a people can govern themselves has been so far worked out, but it is a question and a question of the greatest interest, whether in the altered circumstances in which before many years America will find herself, her democratic institutions will be so effective. She is still in her infancy, her population is small, and is still but one people, but when her population becomes great, and it is increasing with amazing rapidity, when her interests become more complicated and perhaps conflicting, it may be doubted whether the bond of union shall be preserved among the states, and if even one or two should separate from the confederacy, it is difficult to say what important consequences might ensue.

By far the finest part of the United States lies to the West of the Alleghany range, there, the rich vallies of the Ohio and Mississippi offer such inducement to the agriculturist, that the great current of emigration is bending in that direction, and before long there will be many powerful states in that country, extending even to the base of the Rocky Mountains.

There is a marked difference between the Southerns and the people of the Northern and Eastern States. Their feelings, habits etc. from the modification of climate and state of society, are totally different, jealousy already exists between them, and serious dissension is apprehended from the Tariff, the State Question and other matters. Now, I think, it can hardly be expected that the federal Union will be preserved among states occupying such an immense extent of country and differing so widely as they do, in climate, in character, and in their pursuits. It is true, the great facility of speedy intercourse afforded by railroads, canals and rivers, forms a powerful bond. Were it not for these advantages distant states would soon become estranged. The people of the extreme South in a few generations would know as little of the Northerners as the Spaniards do of the Russians.

Having decided on paying a visit to Cuba, we thought it better to proceed there at once, and from thence to New Orleans, in preference to going direct to New Orleans by land. Most of our way by that route would have lain through uninteresting " pine barrens." Besides travelling in Florida and Georgia is now rendered extremely unsafe by scattered parties of hostile Indians, who have been committing much devastation.

We took our passage in a little Spanish Brig called " The Abencessage," and sailed from Charleston on the 12th May, as the Captain and men were Spaniards and not a word of English to be had on board, we provided ourselves with a Spanish Dictionary and Grammar, determined to apply ourselves assiduously to the acquisition of the language. By dint of constant speaking we picked up a good many words, and were soon able to ask for anything we wanted.

The Captain was a very smart looking little fellow. He had an intelligent countenance, polite manners and wore a red *gurro* or Moorish cap, which added to his animated and bronzed features, gave him rather a striking appearance. He seemed to know very little of his profession. The mate was quite a lad, and the most incessant talker I ever heard, he was absolutely possessed of a talking Devil. From morning till night, his tongue never ceased wagging. He used to hold forth to us by the hour, Heaven knows about what. At times he would talk to himself, or take the Dictionary and rattle off whole columns with great emphasis, talking seemed necessary to his existence, he lived but in the sound of his own voice.

Some of the crew were very fine-looking men, tall, spare, muscular fellows. When lying at dinner on the deck, round a dish of Olla Podrida, with long knives stuck in their red sashes and broad sombreros shading their strongly marked features, they presented a very piratical looking group, and as Cuba has always been a favourite rendezvous of pirates, I have no doubt that some of them in their time had practised as " Sea Attornies." They took matters easily, spent most of their time lying on the shady side of the deck, smoked their cigarios, and trusted to San Antonio. He is the Saint in whom Spanish sailors particularly confide, and whom they invoke in all emergencies.

The cabin was a shocking little dog-hole of a place, smelling strongly of a villanous combination of bilge water, garlic and rancid oil. Our meals, pure, unadulterated specimens of Spanish cookery, were served on deck " al fresco." Our live stock con- sisted of the ricketty-looking fowls, as for the rest of our fresh food, it depended on Providence, and our skill in fishing. What our salt meal was, it would have puzzled a wiser head than mine to have discovered. From its consistency and taste, I take it to have been the salted flesh of seahorse.

Garlic and oil were used in unlimited profusion. The savoury smell that rose from the vessel at cooking time must have perfumed the sea for miles around. The water we had was full of reptiles like young sea-serpents, and must have been particu- larly nutritious from the quantity of animal life it contained.

Our attendant was a Lascar boy, who was by no means fastidiously clean in his habits. I have no doubt a fine comb might have been applied to his head with great success. What the original colour of his shirt was, would have been a difficult question to solve. He wore it in an easy unembarrassed manner, outside his trousers, allowing it to flutter freely in the breeze. The advantage of this was, it was eminently useful in several respects, for instance, it served as a napkin ; on changing our plates at dinner, he always wiped the knives and forks on the tail of his shirt.

For a person who had any prejudice in favour of cleanli- ness, it required great resolution to partake of the dishes that were set before us. But we had stout hearts and strong stomachs and acted on the principle of Captain Dugald Dalgetty, always to tuck in our provent when we could get it, and keep the garrison well provisioned.

The first two or three days there was scarcely any wind. The sea was smooth as glass, and the sun blazing hot. Many a prayer was addressed to San Antonio for wind. " Sopla, Sopla, San Antonio " was the universal cry. At last, a fair breeze did come, and as the little Brig was a fast sailer, we got on very well.

One afternoon, the crew were lying as usual on deck, the helm man dozing at the wheel, the mate busy talking and the Captain listening, or appearing to listen, to him. Henry and I were looking over the side when I perceived at the distance of half a cable's length a portion of the water that appeared dark and discoloured. I called Henry's attention to it and said I was sure it was the point of a reef, in a few minutes afterwards the brig struck, and after being bumped some time on the rock, greatly, I should think, to the detriment of her bottom, a sea lifted her up and carried her fairly off but when we looked round, we found we were completely surrounded by reefs, in some places their black points appeared above water with the sea at times breaking over them. How we got out of the difficulty I cannot conceive, it certainly was not by good management. It was very touch and go work, not half a foot of water to spare.

When the brig struck, the Captain did not know what to do. He threw down his cigar, and danced about the deck in a state of great perplexity, calling to his aid every saint in the calendar. The mate for once, held his jaw, and the only one of the crew who shewed any presence of mind was an old skin dried fellow we called Don Quixote, from the close resemblance he bore to the prints of that worthy knight. He went out on the bowsprit, and gave the helmsman directions how to steer.

Several sharks were plunging about, one enormous fellow came up and rubbed against the vessel's side ; they would have had great feasting had we gone down.

The place where we struck is to the Eastward of the Bahama Isles. The navigation there is rendered exceedingly intricate and dangerous, by the great number of sunken rocks. These are long sharp reefs with deep water on each side, and when a vessel strikes, unless she gets jammed, she is apt to fall off and go down at once.

On the evening of the eighth day, we made the high land above Matanzas called the Pau de Matanzas, greatly to the exultation of the Captain, who seemed very proud at having found the island. For all he knew of our exact position the day before, we might as well have made St. Domingo or Jamaica. Next morning on coming on deck, about five o'clock I found we were under the guns of the Fort El Morro, which command the entrance to the harbour of Havana. A British man-of-war was close to us, standing out, with all sails set to catch the light breeze from land. She was a noble object on the waters, looking like a floating castle, while our craft in comparison sank into utter insignificance.

As it was some time before we could work into harbour, we had full time to get a good view of the city, which looks particularly well from sea. It is built along the shore of a semi-circular bay. The points of land at each extremity of the bay are higher than the surrounding country, and strongly fortified. Behind the city, running parallel with the sea, is a range of rather elevated land, interspersed with clumps of tall cocoa-nut and palm trees. The harbour is at the east end of the town, the entrance to it is a narrow gut, running a short way into the land, and there expanding into a beautiful and capacious bason, completely protected from every wind. It has the great advantage that vessels can get in and out at all times of the tide. There is deep blue water up to the very walls of the fort.

No hostile fleet I should think could get in here, provided the batteries were manned by soldiers who would stand to their guns.

After getting into the harbour, a heavy ten-oared barge came along side, and a Custom House Officer boarded us. After receiving our passports, he gave us to understand that we must not land till we obtain express permission from the Governor. It was some time before the old " Don " could make us " sinsible " what he was driving at, but at last we deciphered his meaning, and found that remonstrance was useless, there we must remain till the governor's permission was obtained. There was no use grumbling—if one goes to visit foreign countries one must be content to abide by whatever conditions the authorities may please in their wisdom to impose. " Paciencia, paciencia," said the old gentleman as he bade us " adios." He left us under care of a soldier who mounted guard over us— " Paciencia " indeed, in a stinking little vessel, under a broiling sun and the land within gun-shot of us.

Fortunately, before leaving Charleston, I had got an official note from Wm. Ogilby, to the British Consul at Havana. I sent this letter, with a note to the Consul, begging he would endeavour to procure us permission to land, and waited with great resignation for an answer, but before that came we had plenty of time to take a full view of our position, which presented a very lively prospect. There was much shipping on the harbour, two Spanish men-of-war and a beautiful Yankee frigate were anchored in the middle of the Bason. Boats of all kinds were rowing about, from the stately ten-oared barge with its curtained awning in the stern, down to the little canoe. There were men-of-war boats easily to be distinguished by their neat equipments and the style in which their crews stretched to the oars. Then there were clumsy country boats laden with pineapples, melons, oranges, and other delicious tropical fruits. Several hundred negroes were hard at work on one side of

the harbour at the wharves, and on the other side at the forti-
fication which was being extended, by way of sweetening their
toil, with the charms of melody, they howled forth most
obstreperously a comical up and down see-saw sort of a chant —
and the bells of all the churches in the city seemed to be holding
a general concert, for they were jingling away in full chorus.
The appearance of almost everything was new to me, but what
struck me particularly as foreign looking were the tufted cocoa
trees and the strange palms with their tall smooth stems and
fan-like leaves.

In about two or three hours the Captain returned without an
answer, upon which we came to an understanding with the
sentinel, that we were to get leave of absence on condition of
coming on board at evening. It was a long time before we discovered the Consulate, and many a twist and turn we took
through the narrow streets and often did we retrace our steps.
To all our enquiries, we invariably received the same answers,
" Si, si, Senor," — " Yes, yes, Sir," or " quia Sahe," Who knows?
At last we did succeed in discovering the Consul's residence, he
had not received my letter, consequently had not got permission for us to land. It was, then, he said, too late that day to
apply, for the governor was a very methodical old gentleman,
and appointed certain hours for business, after which he would
sign no paper, if it were to save the island from being swallowed
by an earthquake he might do so, but only on such a pressing
occasion.

The next day being Sunday, it was doubtful whether permission could be had, but he said he would endeavour to procure
it. In the meantime he begged us to dine with him, an invitation
we accepted with much pleasure. Dinner was served in a long
Piazza that extended along one side of a quadrangular court.
There was rather a large party. Mr. Tolme has a very extensive
establishment, and employs a great number of clerks. Fifteen
or twenty of these young bucks, all rigged out in white linen

jackets, sat down to table. Like Louis Kissnigo our " appetize-
ment" was very keen, and the sight of Christian looking fresh
meat was very tempting after the horrid messes of garlic and
oil on which we were fed, on board the brig.

To it we went, with good will, keeping a couple of black
fellows busy attending to our wants. Dinner and the white-
jackets disappeared together. We then adjourned to another
room where wines and segars were produced, the Consul plied
his segar with great assiduity. I followed his example, and
under cover of a cloud of smoke we were soon engaged in an
interesting conversation. We found Mr. T. a very gentlemanlike, well-informed person. According to the agreement with
our Sentinel, we returned on board the brig. Next forenoon,
the Vice Consul came on board with our permission, and then
we made our public entry into the city of Havana, establishing
ourselves at the Posado de la Bella Europa.

Havana is by far the finest town in the West Indies, and
holds a high rank among the commercial cities of the world.
It owes its prosperity, I am told, more to the enterprise of
foreigners than to the exertions of the natives, who are generally of indolent habits. The principal merchants are old
Spaniards. There are also Germans, some Americans, and a few
English.

The streets are very narrow, and the houses, many of which
are large, are constructed in a curious style of architecture,
and with their heavy balconies, barred windows, and studded
gates, present a novel appearance to the stranger, resembling
fortresses more than regular dwellings. The entrance into most
of the houses is through a Porte Cochere, into a quadrangular
court, round which runs a piazza, supported on heavy pillars,
and communicating with extensive suites of apartments. The
rooms are spacious with lofty roofs, and they are encumbered
with as little furniture as possible. The window frames are
formed of thick bars, without glass, as in this warm climate

every breath of wind that blows is too precious to be excluded. During the heat of the day, thick blinds are drawn across to protect the inmates from the rays of the sun.

By day-time few people move out except on business, and then they drive in a whimsical looking vehicle, which is, I believe, peculiar to Havana. It is called a Volante, and is an exaggerated caricature of a cabriolet, with immense wheels at least six feet high. And the animal that draws it (scarcely deserving the name of a horse) with his tail tied tightly to the saddle, is attached to the end of the shafts at such a distance from the body of the vehicle, that he and it appear momentarily about to part company. But the most extraordinary part of the equipage is the black postilion, with his preposterously sized straw hat and his gaudily laced jacket and boots which stand up about half a yard above the knee, with very capacious mouths as if they were intended as buckets to receive the streams of perspiration that flow profusely from his sable face. These boots, or rather leggings, unlike the French Postilion's, fit closely to the leg from the knee to the ankle. The stocking-less foot is furnished with low shoes, and spurs of such formidable dimensions that any prudent horse must tremble to look at them.

Sometimes, during the day, you may see a senora whose age warns her to renounce the pomps and vanities of this wicked world, gliding along the shady side of the street, on her way to church, with a long black veil over her head and shoulders (bonnets are here unknown) and followed by a negro bearing her missal.

But night, and the nights in this climate are delicious, with their deep blue skies and stars whose bright beauty I never felt so powerfully as now, and if the moon be up, she shines, not as in our clime dimly, through clouds and vapour, but from the clear vault of Heaven, pours down her beams in unsubdued splendour, though with such mellow light, as to invest with a tender beauty every object on which they fall—Night is the season for visiting and amusement.

The Placa del Gobernador is crowded with promenaders enjoying the music of a fine military band. Volantes are driving about in all directions, and as you walk along the streets, you may see through the open doors and windows the rooms crowded with company; your ears are regaled with the tinkling of guitars, and every thing you behold presents a scene of gaiety and amusement.

Before the administration of the present Governor, a ramble through the streets of Havana by night was far from safe. The laws were lax, the authorities were corrupt, justice was bartered, a criminal could purchase impunity for any crime, and the consequence was that assassinations were of almost nightly occurrence, and there was little protection for either life or property. But General Tacon, the present Governor in the two years he has presided over the island has effected great changes. His energetic measures have been crowned with complete success and the people of Havana have just reason to be grateful to him. He has caused the laws to be administered promptly and impartially, he has organized an efficient Police, suppressed the gambling houses that were so productive of crime and made great improvements in the streets. Yet he is, I am informed, detested by the Creoles, merely because his administration is conducted with integrity—a corrupt officer is just the man they would like. The salary of the Governor is about six thousand pounds of our money. The predecessor of General Tacon pocketted ten times that sum by bribes, sale of pardons, etc.

From the number of churches and religious houses I should think that Havana contains a formidable array of priests.

The Cathedral is the principal church. It contains the bones of Columbus, which were removed from St. Domingo and deposited in its shrine.

There is a pleasant walk of considerable extent outside the walls, lined with beautiful trees, whose luxuriant foliage affords a grateful shelter from the intense heat of the sun, and whose boughs are loaded with delicious fruit, the golden orange gleams amidst the green leaves and the luscious mango, the clustering cocoa nut and many other tropical fruits abound in unlimited quantity.

Close to the walk is the botanical garden, which is not kept in very good order, but contains some valuable specimens. We there saw the bread-fruit tree in full bearing—the tree from which the Indian rubber is extracted. This substance is a glutinous liquid of milky appearance, which exudes from the bark on being punctured. We also saw coffee plants and mahogany trees, which, however are no rarities here. In this garden is a very beautiful avenue of palm trees—they exactly present the appearance of a long Gothic aisle, their smooth, regular stems form the columns, and their long drooping branches the pointed arches. Hundreds of lizards were darting about in pursuit of insects, mighty dragon flies careered through the air, and gorgeous butterflies, like gay coxcombs, displayed their bright colours and fluttered about from bush to bush, flirting with every fair flower that caught their view.

The Spaniards have introduced here their great national sport of bull fighting, this amusement is conducted with much pomp, and according to the rules of the Spanish circus. It is carried on now with greater spirit than ever. Several eminent Picadors and Matadors have been lately imported from the old country, and their skill has excited great admiration among the amateurs.

We witnessed a grand spectacle of this sort the other day. The Placa de Toros is at a pretty little place called Regla, on the other side of the harbour. On arriving there, we found a vast assemblage of people. The sport is held in a spacious amphitheatre. In the centre is a circular arena, round which

run rows of benches rising tier above tier up to the roof of the
building, capable of accommodating great numbers and affording a full view of the fight to every individual. The seats were
crowded with spectators, among whom were a fair proportion
of ladies. As soon as the Governor appeared in his box, a door
opened and four footmen and two cavaliers entered, and having
paid their obeisance to his Excellency, made the circuit of the
ring. They were dressed in a very picturesque Spanish costume.
The footmen carried short javelins and red scarfs which they
flung into the animal's face to enable them to elude his attack.
At intervals, round the circumference of the ring, were little
barricades to which they might retreat if the bull pressed on
them too closely.

The horsemen were armed with long lances, blunt at the
point and so shaped as to enable them merely to repel the
attack without inflicting a very deep wound.

On a given signal, a door was thrown open, and out rushed a
bull. He stopped for a few moments in the centre of the arena, glaring wildly around him, evidently distracted by the
strangeness of the scene, and the shouts of the spectators. The
footmen advanced and planted two or three javelins in his hide,
he shook his head, bellowed with rage and pain, spurned up
the sand with his hoof, and was evidently preparing for mischief. In an instant he scattered the footmen in all directions,
chasing them round the ring and driving them for shelter
behind the barricades. They had need of all their agility to
effect their escape — he then ran, full tilt at the nearest cavalier,
striking the horse full in the chest with terrible force, down
went man and steed, on dashed the bull against the next horseman who was advancing to the assistance of his fallen comrade.
This man repelled the first charge very steadily, wounding the
animal in the shoulder, however it instantly repeated the
onset and this time the horse rearing with fright was caught

under the breast by the bull's horns and thrown right on his back amidst deafening shouts of "bueno toro"—"good bull."

The footmen now engaged him till the horses were dragged out. One of them was so dreadfully gored that he could not have survived many minutes—the blood was welling from a deep wound in his chest with as much violence as if it had been expelled by a forcing pump. The spectators were in raptures, with the prowess of the bull. Even the gentle senoras uttered expressions of admiration. To the honour of the fair sex, be it told, one young lady who was seated near me, was much shocked. She turned her face shudderingly from the bloody spectacle and exclaiming "Muy terrible," rose, and would have retired, but the old Don, her papa, laughed at her squeamishness, and insisted on her resuming her seat.

After the bull was baited for some time longer the Governor gave the signal for killing him. By this time he was in an awful state of excitement, foam was flying from his mouth, and his eyes glowed like coals of fire. The Matador, a cool steady old fellow holding in one hand a little red flag, and in the other a long straight sword, now advanced in front of the savage beast, which, as if instinctively aware of the presence of a formidable enemy, stood glaring at him a few minutes. Then they stood like two gladiators, who gaze on each other as if measuring their respective strength before closing in deadly encounter. The Matador, to provoke an attack, shook the red flag before him, the bull immediately lowered his head and made a rush, but the old swordsman, just as the horns nearly touched his breast, with wonderful coolness and precision, plunged his weapon up to the very hilt in its neck. The beast instantly stopped, blood gushed from its nostrils, his breast heaved, his limbs quivered convulsively, and after swaying about for a second or two, he sank down in the agonies of death. Three steeds gaily caparisoned were then introduced, and attached

to the carcass, which they dragged out of the arena at full
gallop.

The next bull was still more mettlesome, he dashed into the
circus with great animation, instantly singled out an object of
attack, charged one of the picadors with such hearty good will
that he had him down in a twinkling, burying his horns up to
the very head in the horse's breast and repeating the poke with
great effect. This bull, to his own share, gored three horses and
tossed very handsomely into the air one of the footmen, who,
however, escaped with an awful rent in his yellow silk breeches.
Whether it was from hurt or fright, I do not know, but it was
some time before he could stand without support, he found it
was no joke to have a mad bull playing at shuttlecock with his
carcass.

Six bulls were successively introduced, four of which were
killed, of the two that were not put to death, one was baited
with bloodhounds. These dogs are vicious enough but they have
not the tenacity of grip of the English bulldog. Three horses
were killed and three more seriously wounded.

Indulgence in such barbarous amusements as this must have
a bad effect on the character of the people, thus accustoming
them to sights of blood and cruelty.

After the sports were over, we walked to the top of one of
the hills which nearly surround the harbour. The view from
this was beautiful: the lovely bay running into a deep bosom
among the green hills, the city with its numerous spires, gleaming in the light of the setting sun, the narrow entrance of the
harbour with its strong forts on each side, away in the distance
the glorious blue sea, and around us luxuriant groves of mango
and palm trees all combined to form a landscape of surpassing
loveliness. We remained there till long after sunset, enjoying
the delightful scene. Fire-flies glanced through the still air, the
nightjar circled round our heads uttering its querulous note,
every blade of grass was vocal with the chirrupping of the

" shrill Cicadu," and from the hill where we stood we could mark the course of boats across the harbour, from the phosphorescent flashes caused by the dipping of the oars. It will be long before the beauty of that scene fades from my memory. As we returned through Regla the street was crowded with people enjoying the balmy freshness of the night air.

The rainy and unhealthy season has now set in. We have been fortunate in having had as yet only two wet days. When it does rain, it pours in such torrents as if there was going to be a second edition of the Deluge, accompanied with thunder and lightning. One evening on our voyage here, I had the luck to witness a thunderstorm at sea. The day had been intensely warm, the sun blazing from a clear sky, but towards evening dark clouds began to collect and pile themselves together in heavy masses, that seemed to rest upon the sea.

The water became of a black hue, there was not a breath of wind but an awful stillness in the air that was quite oppressive. We all stood in silence looking at the dark quarter of the heavens, presently along the edge of a black mass of vapour, that was a little detached from the rest, a light flame played for an instant. A deep muttering was heard as if that giant cloud were giving signal to the rest, and then a flash that almost blinded us broke from the gloom, lighting the sea far and wide with its livid glare. A crashing report followed like the simultaneous discharge of ten thousand pieces of artillery. This was but the prelude. Lines of light like fiery snakes kept wriggling and darting from the black clouds, and the rain came down in such torrents as if it would have swamped the vessel.

The weather is very warm. My room happened to be next the cooking shop—a kitchen range adjoins it, which raises the temperature considerably (purgatory will be quite a trifle to this) and makes it the favourite residence of all the vermin of the establishment. Cockroaches, mosquitoes, ants, lizards, etc., seem to consider themselves quite at home, and treat me very

unceremoniously, but " Paciencia, pacienca," as the old Don
said.

There is a comparatively cool room on the opposite side of
the Court, occupied by a gentleman who is to leave in a day or
two, and I am determined to locate myself there.

Sitting at my own door, I can't help seeing into his room, and
observing the quantity of luggage, the portmanteaus, carpet
bags, writing and dressing case. I, at once concluded it must be
an Englishman who had thus carried his comforts with him,
the first time I saw him in the coach, I addressed him in English,
and had the satisfaction of being answered in the same tongue.
We established a visiting acquaintance, and soon got on friendly
terms, greatly to my advantage. He is well provided with books,
which he has placed at my services and, moreover, he wished
to present me with a very handsome thermometer, which I
could not think of accepting from a total stranger. He tells me
he has travelled through most of the continent of Europe, in
America and through many of the West India islands.

20th May. This day there has been a grand procession on
the occasion of carrying about the Host. The streets through
which it passed were lined with troops and covered with
awnings to protect the reverend padres from the sun. The
balconies were crowded with females in their gayest attire.
The streets, and particularly the square in front of the Cathedral, were filled with spectators. It was a very novel sight. The
Host, which was carried in a richly ornamented litter, was
preceded and followed by a long retinue of priests, monks and
friars, of all denominations, in full canonicals. The abbots and
other dignitaries, arrayed in rich robes with cape and stole,
and bearing crosiers. On its approach the troops presented
arms, the people took off their hats and made obeisance, the
drums beat, the trumpets sounded, the cymbals clashed, and
the priests swept on with the mummery. It is by such acts that

an ignorant population is enslaved, their minds are made cap-
tives by their senses.

King craft and priest craft says good William Howitt have
been productive of more evil to the human race than all other
causes combined. Certainly from the days of Nimrod, the first
conqueror, down to the present time, kings and priests have
walked the world together tyrannising over the bodies and
minds of men, and filling the earth with tears and blood. But
so must it be till mankind be regenerated by the influence of
knowledge. Better that the mass should groan under the most
cruel despotism, than be without government; better that they
should be devotees of the most superstitious creed, than be
without a religion.

As mankind are at present, I fear that the majority of them
are only fit to be slaves, but the human mind is asserting its
power. The world is fast improving, and old things are passing
away, yet slow must be the process through which it will pass
to a state of universal enlightenment and liberty.

At the procession I was much amused by the gay attire of
the black ladies, and by the conscious air of finery which they
exhibited. How they strutted and bridled and flirted their large
fans and held high their heads, and gazed about them with a
look which plainly said, " See how very fine I am." They were
generally dressed in white, which formed a pleasing contrast
to their dusky complexions. White veils fastened to the crown
of the head fell over their shoulders ; their necks were loaded
with chains, their arms with bracelets, and their fingers with
rings. Their comically made legs were cased in silk stockings,
and their outlandish looking feet were squeezed into very gay
satin shoes. They seemed to pay much attention to this part
of their dress. The prevailing colours of their shoes were bright
yellow, bright blue, and bright red.

I remarked one poor girl—she was dressed in a dirty old
calico gown, about the same dimensions as the Cutty Sark,

that makes such a figure in Tam O'Shanter, and the only piece
of finery she had was a pair of yellow satin shoes on her
stockingless feet. The love of dress appears to be inherent in
the female breast. The sable belle of Africa has just as great
a passion for gay attire as the fair beauty of Europe. The ladies
of the North American Indians are very curious and careful in
the choice and adjustment of the human scalps, porcupine
quills, bears' teeth etc., with which they ornament their scanty
robes, and I have no doubt if one paid a visit to Lapland, one
would find some dames of consideration and importance in
each community who set the fashion and lead the " ton."

I was surprised at the manner in which some of the Negro
females were dressed, but was told that among the free blacks,
there are many in comfortable circumstances.

The Spanish laws are more favourable to the slaves than
the laws that obtained in the English West India colonies. A
slave has the right of changing his master. If he can prove that
he was barbarously treated, he may also insist on purchasing
his freedom whenever he is able to pay his value, and an
industrious negro after performing his allotted task, has generally time to work for himself. Besides, it is the custom for many
slaves to provide employment for themselves and pay a certain
daily sum to their masters. Whatever they can make over and
above, belonging to themselves. Many families are thus supported by their Negroes. The number of free blacks in the island
proves how extensively they have availed themselves of this
privilege of purchasing their liberty. In 1823 the population

	Whites	Free Cod.		Slaves
of Cuba was ...	715,000	325,000	130,000	260,000
of Jamaica ...	402,000	25,000	35,000	342,000
United States...	10,525,000	8,575,000	285,000	1,665,000

By this census it appears that the population of Cuba is

nearly double that of Jamaica, with the advantage of having a much greater population of whites.

In spite of the activity of our cruisers, the accursed slave trade is still carried on briskly. Seventy slavers belong to the Port of Havana alone, and immense numbers of these unfortunate wretches are annually brought to the island. The mortality among them is very great, particularly if they arrive in the months of June, July and August.

In the course of thirty years from 1790 to 1820, 372,449 were imported to Havana. When we compare the present number with the annual importation we may form some estimate of the mortality that prevails. A treaty was concluded between England and Spain to the effect that the slave trade should be prohibited North of the Equator from November 1817, and that it should be entirely abolished in May 1820, Spain receiving from Great Britain £400,000 as compensation for the loss she might sustain. Yet, in spite of this treaty, the authorities here, if they do not encourage the abominable traffic, allow slave vessels openly to be fitted out in their ports.

Cuba is the largest of all the West Indian Isles, with the exception perhaps of St. Domingo, but its riches are yet unexplored. The interior of the country is little known, and it is only along some parts of the coast that cultivation has extended.

The soil generally of an undulating surface, is fruitful. There are few mountains, the principal elevations are the Pan de Matanzas, Arcos de Canasi and Siena de Cobre. Being on the verge of the torrid zone, the summers are scorching hot, but the winters, I am informed, are most delightful.

Cuba is possessed of most important advantages. Both from the long narrow shape of the island, presenting an extensive development of coast, thickly indented by safe harbours, which can be easily communicated with from all parts of the interior, and also from its very position lying as it does at the entrance

to the Gulf of Mexico, within a short sail of St. Domingo,
Jamaica, the Antilles, the southern part of the United States,
and the northern coast of Mexico. If it were in the hands of an
enterprising people, and free from the curse of slavery, it
would become a most important country, rich in its own
resources and capable of carrying on an extensive commerce.
As it is, it is prospering. Its principal mart, Havana, is rapidly
improving. In the last twenty years it has doubled its population, being an increase equal to that of New York. The principal exports are sugar, coffee, tobacco, fruit, some indigo and
cotton.

The aborigines of Cuba, have long since disappeared. The
Spaniards, with that ferocious spirit of extermination which
distinguished all their conquests in the New World, butchered
the natives. At the time of its conquest, 1511, it contained a
million of inhabitants. Six years afterwards in 1517, there were
left only 14,000. Of all the vast colonial possessions of Spain,
Cuba is almost the only one that acknowledges her sway, and
I think the time is not very far distant when it will also be
lost to her.

The Creoles have no very cordial feeling to the old country.
The only thing that prevents their at once asserting their
independence is the apprehension of an insurrection among the
blacks. The fate of the Spanish colonies in South America, and
of the English colonies in North America, presents a curious
illustration of the character and habits of the two nations, both
separated from the mother countries, animated ostensibly by
the same motives ; but while the calm steadiness of purpose,
the enlightened love of liberty, the commercial enterprise and
industrious habits of the Anglo Americans have commanded
for their country the respect of foreign powers and secured
domestic peace and unprecedented prosperity, the career of
the Spanish Americans has been quite the reverse, passing from
revolution to revolution, distracted by violent and bloody dis-

sensions. Public order is held by an uncertain tenure, and public prosperity is based upon very insecure foundations.

What the future condition of the West Indies may be, is a subject that affords much interesting speculation, hitherto they have but ministered to the cupidity of Europeans, they have been acquired by blood, retained at a great expense of lives, and made productive by compulsory labour. The entire colonial system was founded in oppression. Owing to the manly policy of the British Government a new era has now commenced. The black population of the English colonies will soon be free. All restraints on their intellectual improvement will be removed. With their freedom the next generation will acquire free sentiments and self respect and will be able properly to appreciate their true position.

When we take into consideration the total black population of all the islands, forming as they do such a great majority, their rapid increase in proportion to the whites, and the spread of information among them, the question naturally arises, " Can the present state of things continue?" " Can these fertile and beautiful islands, be retained by Europeans much longer?" West Indian proprietors may despise the blacks and laugh at the idea of their ever making a successful movement, yet they should consider that henceforward the Negroes will be placed in totally different circumstances. They will be free labourers receiving proper remuneration for their industry, and all restraints on education being removed, their moral condition must necessarily improve amazingly. Now this will render the European sway insecure.

It would be a curious dispensation of Providence and one not at all unlikely, if the descendants of these unfortunate people, who have been led captive from their native land, should be destined to expel their taskmasters, and of these beautiful islands, to whose climate they are better adapted than the whites, form a confederation of free states.

June 1836

6th June. At another bullfight—four bulls killed—four or five horses dreadfully mangled, yet as long as they could stand the picadors kept spurring them round the course, though their entrails were hanging down almost to the ground.

I am surprised how the horsemen escaped, both from the bulls' horns and from the severe falls they had and the horse often falling back over them and rolling over them. The bandevilleros displayed extraordinary agility. One of them when the bull had his horns lowered to toss him and his fate seemed inevitable, somehow made a side hop over the animal's head and escaped.

Yellow breeches, who nearly lost his life last fight, kept at a prudent distance and took particularly good care of himself. This bullfighting is a shockingly cruel amusement, and such as none but a cruel people would patronise, but the Spanish character is very sanguinary. It has always shown itself to be so. Never were such horrible atrocities committed as in their conquest of the New World, and at the present time, the exterminating system on which the war in Spain is conducted is disgraceful to humanity.

Man is a curious compound; something of the God, something of the Devil and a great deal of the Brute.

16th June. Out today for the first time after an attack of fever owing, I suppose, to my not calling in a doctor. I am recovering rapidly. The first day I was unwell, the waiters gathered round my bed, and said that, from the symptoms, it was yellow fever, which is a very fatal disease, particularly to Europeans. I was attacked by excruciating pains in my head, back and limbs, and the blood flowed through my veins like

73

liquid fire. Harry and I held a consultation and decided on a mode of treatment which proved very successful. I thought I had a better right to make experiments on myself than any Spanish doctor. Tomorrow we sail for N. Orleans.

   17th. Once more on the blue waters — a bright joyous day with just wind sufficient to fill the sails and make the sea sparkle. El Morro has faded in the distance, the palm-covered hills are each moment growing more dim and indistinct, scarcely to be distinguished over the wave, and now they are gone. I have taken my last look at Cuba. Our vessel is the schooner Player commanded by Davy Jones, a very ominous name, by-the-bye to go to sea with. There are twenty-seven passengers on board. Among them are representatives of almost every European nation, English, Irish, Scotch, French, Spanish, Portuguese, Italian and Germans, and to wind up the collection, there is a large assortment of parrots and poodle dogs. You may conceive what a Babellike confusion of tongues there is. The decks are so crowded with baskets of fruit, we have scarcely room to move.

   The super cargo, and part proprietor of the vessel is a Yankee, a smooth tongued, canting, swindling Yankee. He shamefully cheated a crazy French sailor, who had a bag of 500 dollars with him, the hard-won earnings of years. The Yankee persuaded this poor fellow to purchase some fruit from him at an exorbitant price. This was on a Sunday, and immediately after doing so, he called for his Bible and read two or three chapters with great devotion, saying that he had been piously brought up, and that religion to him was the most precious treasure on earth.

   The Yankees have obtained for themselves a very unenviable notoriety. They are very strict in all ceremonial observances, but it is said they neglect the weightier matters of the law. The New England states produce a peculiar class of people called Yankee Pedlars. They are a race " sui generis." Keen sharp-witted fellows, with great volubility and an infinite stock of impudence, they generally travel about with a light one-horse wagon, containing an assortment of *notions*, and some of these notions are such as could have emanated only from the inventive brain of a Yankee. They sell dress and trinkets for women, toys for children, clocks of a peculiar construction *made for sale*, wooden nutmegs and melon seed manufactured of the pith of some tree. They are in the habit of making forays into some of the Southern and Western States, and bearing off rich spoil. The people of some districts, however, so heartily detest these Yankee Pedlars that if one has the temerity to enter their borders to practise his tricks, he is sure to be lynched.

Dead calm for eight days, amused ourselves fishing for dolphin, quantities of which sometimes come round the vessel, they are beautiful fish in the water, and when dying, in their changes of colour, they display all the tints of the rainbow.

One day a shark was caught, it was attended by two pilot fish, pretty little things, marked on the back like mackerel. When the shark was hauled up almost to the surface of the water, the pilot fish kept swimming right over him, so near as almost to touch. Sailors say, the shark will not take a bait till the pilot has examined it and reported on it. Skin of the shark very hard. This one was struck three times with a harpoon without being penetrated.

Arrived at the Balize, the mouth of the Mississippi River, on the fifteenth day from the departure from Havana, South West. The principal passage-depth of water on the bar is from eleven to fifteen feet. The Mississippi water may be easily distinguished sixty miles at sea; keeps longer on board ship than any other water. Very good to drink when the mud subsides. Vessels often run in within a mile or two of shore and procure a supply of fresh water from the river stream, that floats on the surface of the sea. From Balize to New Orleans 104 miles, towed up by a steamer; country on each side swamp and jungle; flocks of pelicans hovering about, alligators in the river.

Mosquitoes and ganninippers attacked us in such force that the passengers were nearly frantic — within four or five miles of the city the sugar plantations commence. New Orleans seated on a bend of the river, well built town. Place of great trade, exports last year seventy-seven millions of dollars. It will be one of the first, if not the first commercial city in the world, situate near the mouth of a mighty river, which, in its course of 4,000 miles, waters a territory of inexhaustible fertility and whose tributaries open up the wide regions of the far West to commercial enterprise. New Orleans possesses amazing advantages which are only beginning to be developed.

Louisiana purchased from the French republic for fifteen millions of dollars. Mr. Adams wished to exchange it with the British Government for the fisheries of Newfoundland. Mr. Clay's policy, however, prevailed. State of society in New Orleans very bad. It is the resort of the most abandoned characters in the United States. Murders in the streets are common and little notice taken of them. The laws are so feebly administered that almost every offence against the person passes unpunished. The principal population is French. It is only lately that the Americans have made an inroad there, and they are looked upon by the original colonists as intruders. The two parties do not draw together well.

Some of the leading merchants in the city are Irishmen, they and the French agree very well, intermarry and keep on the most intimate terms. New Orleans is the place for making money rapidly. If a person once gets fairly started in business he is sure of realizing a handsome independence in the course of a very few years, provided he escapes yellow fever, which is the scourge of this place. From its situation, lying as it does in the midst of swamp, it cannot be but unhealthy. The soil on which it is built is so wet that if you dig two feet deep, water springs up. One cannot get even a dry grave in the ground, the only way they have of burying people comfortably is by building them up in a wall. We visited the cemetery, a most miserable imitation of Père la Chaise. It is a melancholy looking place, a few weeping willows droop mournfully over tombs that are erected without any pretence to taste. Rank weeds grow over the walks and graves, hundreds of loathsome reptiles crawled about, and the noisome effluvia of stagnant water tainted the air. The genius of yellow fever presided over the place. To add to the scene, an old negro who was working at a grave like an ill boding raven, croaked forth a most unearthly ditty which sounded strangely in that lonely place of the dead.

The public buildings of New Orleans are scarcely worth notice, except the Spanish Cathedral which looks very well, particularly from the river. It will be long before the country about the city be thoroughly drained and reclaimed, it is now a curious thing to see, within two miles of a populous mart, the wild uncultivated forest.

It is calculated that each year two thousand flat boats come down the waters of the Mississippi, laden with bacon, flour, whiskey, tobacco, horses, black cattle, etc. The farmers are in the habit of clubbing together, building a flat, bringing their produce to market, selling cargo and boat, and returning home by the steamers.

Steam is the great power by which that immense tract of country lying between the Mississippi and the Rocky Mountains will be civilized. The numerous navigable rivers that having their source in the Rocky Mountains blend themselves with the Mississippi, are by the aid of steam so many high ways by which the arts and comforts of civilized life will be conveyed to the now unexplored wilderness.

Before the introduction of steam navigation on the Western waters, all goods had to be brought up the river from N. Orleans in boats towed by the hands of men, and it then took two or three months to accomplish the distance that is now performed in the same number of weeks. Common labourers' wages at N. Orleans, two dollars a day. Soil of Louisiana, a rich alluvial deposit, inexhaustible, principal and most valuable crops, sugar and cotton. If a plantation has an average crop of sugar every third year he considers himself well paid.

The sugar cane is planted in March and April, in planting it the canes are laid down longitudinally, from every knot a young plant springs up. In the latter end of September and October it is ready for cutting; this is the most critical period, for if the crop is late and the slightest frost comes on, it is ruined. Immediately on being cut, it is carried to the mill to be bruised, next put into the boilers, and after being sufficiently boiled, it is thrown into large vats perforated at the bottom. The sugar, in the process of sweating, purifies itself from the molasses.

The cotton grows on low shrubs planted in March; in September the berries are fully bursted and ready for picking.

July 1836

8th July. Left New Orleans for Louisville by the steamer Pittsburgh. The American steamers as they are adapted to the smooth water of rivers are constructed quite differently from ours; they draw little water, have generally three decks and are raised such a height above the water that they look more like floating houses than vessels. On the Upper deck in the forward part of the vessel, the helmsman is perched in a little glass house, it is necessary he should be so elevated that he may clearly see his course and be enabled to avoid the numerous snags and stumps which render the navigation of the Mississippi dangerous.

Steamboat accidents are of very frequent occurrence in the Western waters; scarcely a month passes without a boat being blown up, burned down, or sunk. We passed four or five wrecks on our passage up the river. These boats are constructed very hastily, of bad materials badly put together. The Americans are always in such breathless hurry that they will not take time to do things permanently. I was informed that many a steamboat had been launched whose timbers ninety days before were uncut in the forest, and whose ironwork was unfashioned in the dark mine. To use their own words, they do go ahead, though sometimes they get along too fast as their steamboat disasters testify. The engines are of the high pressure kind and as they extend under the cabin deck, if they should happen to burst, the passengers are sure to be blown sky high. Considering the flimsy state of the boilers, the carelessness of the engineers, and the spirit of emulation which prompts the captains to race against other boats, not to mention the danger of fires, and the snags and stumps which abound in the Mississippi, it is more likely that you should meet with an accident than that you should perform your voyage in safety. Something went wrong with our machinery which caused considerable alarm for some time.

One meets with a very strange collection of people in a Western steamer. On board the Pittsburgh were about 300 passengers, some of whom were very curious specimens of their kind, such scrambling for places as there was at meal times, such unaccommodating, take-care-of-myself spirit characterized every individual that in self defence we were obliged to be as rude and rough as our neighbours. The *Gentlemen* passed most of their time in gambling, and while they were engaged in this occupation, the wanton imprecations and shocking blasphemy that were bandied round the tables were absolutely disgusting. The whole scene appeared to me to realize the idea of " Hell afloat." The morals of the Southern and Western people seem to be at a very low ebb. As far as I have had an opportunity of judging, they are a gambling, drinking, swearing set of profligates. I heard more blasphemy in the course of one day in New Orleans than I heard during my whole life before.

The distance from N. Orleans to Louisville is thirteen hundred miles. There is this extent of almost uninterrupted forest, wild, savage forest, so dense, and with the trees growing in such rank luxuriance and so closely laced together, that the sunbeams never penetrate the gloom. These woods, particularly at night, present the appearance of solemn, gloomy magnificence, as if they were the lone and secret places of Nature, into which it would be almost profanation for a human foot to intrude.

The gloomy forest impresses on my heart the feeling of solitude far more powerfully than the wild mountain does. On the mountain you have the free air around you, and the blue sky over you. Every thing you see conspires to rouse the spirits, and to give you the idea of liberty, but the gloomy desolateness of the forest has an awe-inspiring effect on the heart, and makes you feel you are indeed alone.

Along the banks of the river are some embryo cities, destined no doubt to become places of importance. Several of them are very classical as far as name goes. Instead of being known by the beautiful and appropriate Indian names of the places, they have been called after the mighty places of old. This is a favourite custom in America. We stopped at Troy, a place which, though not so large, could not, I think, have been surpassed by its ancient namesake in beauty of situation — at Memphis, and at Carthage City, consisting of eight log cabins.

Passing along the river, one occasionally sees a woodman's hut, with a patch of Indian corn adjoining. A squatter comes into the wilderness with little more than his rifle and axe, he sets to work, fells some trees, erects a log house, which is easily constructed, clears a small patch of land that supplies him with maize and sweet potatoes. He is well versed in woodcraft, and while there is game in the forest, he will not want. He soon has an abundance of the necessaries of life. The river supplies him with fish, with his rifle he can procure plenty of venison and bears' meat. The maple affords him sugar. If he takes the trouble to split wood he gets a ready sale for it from the steamboats on the river at the rate of three dollars a load. He has all he wants, plenty to eat and drink, and savage independence. Amenable to no law, he wanders where he pleases, he is not troubled with neighbours; he does not like to be *crowded*, as he says. If any settlement is made within ten miles of him, he is apt to shoulder his rifle and look out for a quieter home. These fellows are far more uncivilised than the Indians. The Indians are gentle, placable beings compared with them. They combine the worst vices of civilization, with those of savage life. They are wild untamed men to use their own expression, of the breed half-horse, half-alligator, and a touch of the earthquake.

The scenery of the Ohio River is much more picturesque than that of the Mississippi. The banks are of a more diversified character, consisting in some places of sloping green hills, at others of rugged cliffs, and precipitous rocks, and in many instances wooded points running out into the stream, seem at a distance to bar it across so that on turning each point you appear to be entering a succession of beautiful lochs.

12th. On the twelfth arrived at Louisville, one of the most flourishing towns of the West. It contains about 20,000 inhabitants. Its natural advantages are very great, being the depot of the produce of an immense tract of fine country. It promises to be one of the largest cities of the United States. Stopped there three days, started for Frankfort, outside the stage, soon found it required considerable ingenuity to ride outside an American stage. The great lumbering vehicle went rolling and pitching, pitching and jolting, at a most confounded rate over roads, the very sight of which would throw Mr. MacAdam into convulsions. They have a kind of road in America, called natural roads, which being interpreted, means no road at all.

Some of the turnpike roads are good enough, but these natural roads are the most unnatural places in the world to venture a coach and four horses, to say nothing of the necks of the passengers. It would make one of the bang up English coachmen stare to see how their American brethren of the whip manage driving through woods and swamps, dashing at every obstacle with desperate temerity, crossing rivers, thundering down rugged hills, with the leaders running wide and wild as if they had eloped from the coach. When I came to pick my seat, and looked at the coarse clumsy accoutrements, and the vehicle itself more like a covered dust cart than a machine for conveying Christian men and women to their destination, I could not help contrasting it with the English post coaches, so neat and commodious, with well groomed horses, polished harness, and everything about them perfectly well regulated. However, to do the American coaches justice, they drive boldly and well, and their machines are better fitted for the rough roads over which they have to travel than the English coaches, which would soon be shaken to pieces.

Picked up at Shelby Ville a comical old Irishman, or as he called himself an Irish Frenchman, he had come up in the boat with us from New Orleans where he had gone in pursuit of a young son, who had run off with the intention of joining the Texans. This gentleman's name was Mister Michael O'Hogan. He had a most mellifluous Munster brogue, great fluency of speech, a fertile imagination, and told lies with uncommon volubility. " Well gentlemen," said he, on mounting the coach, " I'm proud and happy to see you again, by my sowl I may well say happy, for it's delighted I am to find myself out of that thief of a steamboat and on the dacent dry land again, for says I to myself, says I, it would be a sore thing if the Devil should catch me before I got home, for after all my adventures in battle, it would be by no manes a dignified mode of exit, to be blown up in an ould steamboat." We asked him about his adventures, which he was nothing loath to relate, according to which he had served in the French, English, and American armies, in the latter of which he had performed such prodigies of valour at the battle of North Point that he was made a colonel—" and now gentlemen," said he, " I have left the field of glory, and turned my sword into a reaping hook. I am a farmer, a magistrate, and am to be sheriff next year. Maybe they'll make me President yet, for you see, I make spaches to the people and am a great man entirely." So much for Mr. O'Hogan.

The drive from Louisville to Frankfort was through a beautiful country. Woodland and meadow and cornfield are so combined as to form most picturesque scenery. One has at the same time in view the glowing magnificence of the forest and the smiling and cheerful beauties of cultivation, by their contrast they naturally add charms to each other. It is a country the sight of which may well gladden the heart of man.

Situation of Frankfort very romantic, on the Kentucky River in a deep valley, surrounded by lofty wooded hills, banks of the river very beautiful rising to the elevation of four or five hundred feet. No place in America has pleased me so much as this. Here we have been a fortnight, wandering along the cliffs and through the woods, and here I could remain for months exploring this beautiful country before the winter sets in.

But in execution of the plan I have proposed I have many hundred miles to travel through wild and difficult country before the winter sets in. I hope before six weeks are over to be among the Indians of the North West. Was present at a review of the Militia, held for the purpose of raising volunteers to send against the Indians of the South West. This is ostensibly the object, but I have no doubt it is with the ultimate intention of assisting the Texans.

Before long the Yankees will make their way into South America. I think that is clear. The majority are a speculating, vagabondising race, without any local attachments and their spirit of enterprise, love of gain, and grasping disposition will drive them to the South.

The appearance of the Militia did not give me a very high idea of their discipline — in fact their ideas of independence are such, that it would be impossible to make good disciplined soldiers of them.

The colonel in command, having first read General Gaines' letter, calling for volunteers, proceeded to address them. To tell the truth the gallant colonel did not present a very soldierlike appearance. He wore a round hat, a blue uniform coat with a pair of prodigious silver epaulets. His unstrapped trousers had gradually worn up above his boots, displaying a portion of his muscular limbs. Sword belt, he had none, but he had very ingeniously contrived to stick his sword through a surcingle that passed over the saddle. He was mounted on a very fine-looking, high-spirited horse, which, however, he did not sit with the ease and grace of a true cavalier.

The day was intensely hot, and the flies were so annoying that they caused the horse to be very uneasy, and every kick and plunge he gave seriously deranged the equilibrium of the worthy officer. Having, at last, brought his charger to a stand-still, with a black fellow holding the rein to keep him quiet, the colonel proceeded to the business of the day. He first stuffed a lump of tobacco into his mouth, then taking off his hat, he drew from it a piece of paper containing the heads of the speech that he intended to deliver. He then cleared his throat, squirted out a mouthful of tobacco juice, and giving strict injunctions to the Negro to keep the horse steady, he thus commenced:

" Gentlemen, ahem, ahem, gentleman, I say, these are awful times, awful and critical times they are, gentlemen (damn your blood, you black rascal, keep the beast steady). Gentlemen, when I consider and reflect, and take into consideration and reflection the state of our South West frontier, I feel in my breast emotions of such a mighty, powerful and undulating character, I say undulating character, that I'm blowed if I can give expression to them — therefore, gentlemen, therefore (keep the horse steady, you nigger.)" The orator here paused to spit, looked at his manuscript and resumed in a strain of impassioned eloquence to which it is impossible to do justice. The effect of his oration was such that a good many young men stepped forward and volunteered.

At a public dinner, or barbican, given by Mr. Crittenden, held in a wood, great crowd, liberty, and equality, were the order of the day. A sturdy independent yeomanry composed the majority of the party. Would that Ireland had such a yeomanry! Much speechifying of course, the Americans are fond of oratory. If they get quantity they are not very particular

about quality provided it be in the high heroic style. Sound and
bombast take wonderfully. The speaker talked much of the
chivalry of Kentucky—such a word to apply to Americans.

The Governor of Kentucky was present. Some one called on
him for a song. Well, thought I, this is good. What comes next?
To my utter surprise and irrepressible merriment, his Excellency the Governor, the highest executive power in the Com-
monwealth, got up on a table, a long, weazel shaped comical
looking gentleman he was, and sang out at the pitch of a
" skirling " voice, " Draw the Sword, Scotland," suiting the
action to the word, and the word to the action with proper
emphasis and discretion, amid the applauding yells of his half
intoxicated audience. I pictured to myself the indignation and
astonishment that would have been depicted on the countenance of one of our County Lieutenants, if at some public
meeting a freeholder had called on him for a song—to say
nothing of what the Lord Lieutenant of Ireland would do, or
say, if such a request were preferred to him. But they manage
matters differently in this country. The people elect to every
situation and the authorities must court and flatter their
constituents.

Kentucky is a very fine state—climate, salubrious—soil, rich,
based on limestone. It has abundance of iron and coal. By means
of the Ohio River, has a cheap and ready mode of sending its
produce to the great mart of the South. Yet with all its advantages the population is not increasing so rapidly as one would
expect. Many of its inhabitants, not satisfied with the super-
abundant fruitfulness of their own country, sell their property
and join the tide of emigration that is rapidly setting towards
the immense territory that lies further to the West. They leave
their own cultivated fields for the wilds of Illinois and Missouri.

Kentucky was settled about the year 1782. It is really astonishing to consider that the place where I now sit, which little
more than fifty years ago was the haunt of the wild beast and

wandering Indian, is now a thriving town inhabited by people possessed of all the comforts of civilization — with such amazing rapidity does everything progress here.

This country of Kentucky was formerly so valuable to the Indians from the immense quantity of game it produced that there were no permanent settlements made in it by the natives. It was entirely reserved as a hunting ground, and was often the scene of bloody battles between hostile tribes who chanced to cross each other in the chase. The herds of buffaloes that were to be found on the hills and through the cane brakes of this region, are said to have been almost countless. To this day their track to the salt ticks is quite distinct and when their course lay through passes in the hills where the herd was crowded closer together, the ground is beaten down hard and firm like a high road. There is a track of this description, not far from this, extending the distance of fifteen or twenty miles to a salt spring called Big Bone tick, and averaging in breadth about fifty yards. Close to this spring have been found immense Mammoth remains. Others also have been found in the cave on the Green River, together with human bones of such extraordinary size, that estimating the height of the individuals to whom they belonged, according to the present proportion of men, some of them must have been fifteen feet high. This, to be sure, sounds like a Yankee story. It seems something akin to the Great Sea serpent tale, but it is fact. The bones are preserved in a museum, and any one may satisfy himself. The existence of such gigantic men at one period is not harder of credit than to believe that there were animals of the elephant species on the earth, four times larger than the breed of the present day, and of this we have ocular demonstration in the perfect skeletons that have been found.

The first white men who penetrated these wildernesses with the intention of forming a settlement must have been a bold and enterprising band. They were few, but brave and determined. They had to contend not only against the difficulties of the country but against the continual attacks of the Indians. They were shot down at their work, their houses were burned over their heads, their wives and children were scalped. Yet, although often almost exterminated, though often on the verge of ruin, they persevered, got fresh recruits from home, and at last succeeded in settling the State and expelling the Indians, who, strongly attached to their ancient hunting grounds, disputed every spot of land with desperate obstinacy. There are numbers alive who fought in those conflicts, and who can tell many interesting stories of Indian warfare. An old woman who resides here, as illustrating the scenes of strife and blood in which she passed her youth and early womanhood, says she used to think the most beautiful sight she ever saw was a young man dying a natural death in bed. It was the first and only death of the kind she saw for years, and the quietness and peace in which his spirit parted was such a contrast to the violent and terrible deaths she was constantly witnessing, that it struck her as being inexpressibly calm and beautiful.

Mr. C. told me a story of an Indian conflict. Twenty young Indian warriors made a vow that they would advance into Kentucky four or five days' march and do all the injury they could to the settlers. They accordingly crossed the Ohio River, penetrated the country with their characteristic secrecy and caution, and having committed great depredations, and taken many white scalps, turned back towards their own country. However they were chased. Twenty-five Kentuckians were following diligently on their trail. On the fourth or fifth morning the pursuers came up, having for some time observed the trail very fresh, they moved cautiously along and on turning the bend of a hill, they discovered the Indians within shot, seated round a fire. They had killed a buffalo and were just preparing their breakfast. The white men immediately delivered their fire and rushed at them. The Indians sprang up and after

gazing an instant at their enemies, walked slowly and deliberately away, till the whites were within a few paces. They then
wheeled round, delivered their fire with murderous precision
and drawing their tomahawks dashed among them with tremendous yells. This hand to hand conflict continued but a short
time. It was, however, very bloody while it lasted. The com-
batants scattered and each man got behind a tree. By this mode
of fighting, the skirmish was protracted for some time, but the
result was that only three white men escaped. The Indians, of
whom also very few survived the conflict, succeeded in keeping
the field and taking upwards of twenty scalps. This story was
told to Mr. C. by one of the whites who escaped.

Kenton, one of the early settlers, related a Mazeppa-like
adventure he once had. He and two companions crossed the
Ohio for the purpose of stealing horses from the Indians. Having
reached the vicinity of an Indian village unobserved, they lay
concealed in the bush till midnight, then creeping cautiously
along they came to an enclosure where the horses were kept
and taking out as many as they thought they could manage
led them quietly out of the village, then mounting, they rode
for their lives as they knew well that the theft would be
discovered early in the morning and that they should be hotly
pursued. Having ridden with scarce a halt, on the evening of
the next day they arrived at the Ohio. It was too dark and
stormy to cross over that night and, much to their chagrin,
they were obliged to wait till next morning. When day broke
they attempted to cross, but the wind was high and the water
was blown into the horses' nostrils which caused them to rear.

The riders were dismounted and the horses swam back to the
shore. The men followed them and attempted to get them back
without success. At last, Kenton, mortified at his bad fortune,
sat down sullenly on a log by the river side. One of his companions was sitting beside him, the other had gone into the
wood to try to catch one of the horses. Kenton says he some-

how had a suspicion that the Indians were not far off. He heard a slight snapping of rotten sticks and just as he turned round his head towards the direction from whence the sound proceeded, several rifles were discharged. He was untouched but his comrade fell dead beside him. Immediately fifty or sixty Indians jumped out of the bush and surrounded him. Kenton's first impulse was to fly, but seeing escape impossible, and knowing that if he showed any symptoms of apprehension he should lower himself in the eyes of his captors, he assumed a composure he did not feel, and sat on quietly unmoved, looking straight before him, without turning his head either to the right or left. The Indians seated themselves round him and looked at him for some time in silence. At last a young warrior rose and made a speech. Speaking with much energy, and with a strong expression of humour in his countenance, the effect of the address was to make the old warriors unbend their features and smile sedately, while the young men laughed outright and seemed to be amazingly tickled at what he said.

Poor Kenton well knew from the glances directed at him that the mirth was all at his expense, but what the result of the merriment was to be, he could not conceive. He was not kept long in suspense — some of the Indians bounded away laughing into the forest, and soon returned with a wild looking colt they had caught. On the back of this untamed steed they bound Kenton, tied his hands behind his back his legs under the animal's body, passed a wild vine round his neck and fastened him fore and aft to the horse's tail and neck so as to keep him in an upright position and prevent him swaying backwards and forwards. Having thus made him fast, they loosed the horse " with a sudden lash " and poor Kenton soon found himself careering through the forest at a fearful speed, and in momentary dread of having his brains knocked out against the branches. The Indians were greatly amused at his distress, and seemed to enjoy very much the appropriate punishment they had inflicted on his crime. They drove him before them, till they reached their village, they then freed him from the courser on which he had taken such a wild ride. He was in a lamentable condition, one of his arms was broken and his flesh was dreadfully lacerated.

They treated him with great kindness, dressed his wounds, fed him well, and attended him carefully till he had recovered his strength. They then took him further into the country to another of the villages. Some time after, fearing that they intended to torture him at the stake, he determined to attempt his escape, in which he succeeded after incredible hardships.

August 1836

Henry went to pay a visit to Colonel Steele. I had a letter from Judge Porter begging me to meet him at Lexington. Mr. Crittenden and I set off there, spent several very pleasant days with Mr. C., Mr. P., and Mr. Clay. Mr. Clay is the most distinguished man in America — he is a splendid orator, a profound statesman and a most useful country gentleman. His high character commands the respect of his enemies. Few deny that of all Americans, he is the best qualified to possess the Presidential Chair and if any dangerous crisis were to occur, he of all Americans is the man to whom the nation would look, and in whose genius and energy it would confide. It is disgraceful to the Americans that he is not President. It is mortifying to think that they should espouse the claims of a superannuated soldier of moderate capacity, and of an intriguing, trading politician, while they have such a man as Henry Clay among them.

Mr. Clay is a tall, thin, gentleman-like man with a benevolent cast of countenance — fine forehead, small bright grey eyes, often expressive of humour, and a mouth formed for uttering big words. His residence is just what I expected. The grounds are kept in very good order. The house of moderate size is furnished plainly and comfortably, there is no display of wealth but the material and arrangement of everything show it is under the control of a simple and correct taste. He takes great delight in his farm and certainly he has reason to feel very proud of the important advantages which his exertions and example have conferred on this section of Kentucky. To him are owing an improved system of farming, an introduction of new crops and a superior breed of cattle. He spared no expense to confer these benefits on his country. He has imported English horses, best English black cattle, Minno sheep, and asses from Spain.

Few public men of the present day possess more solid and unsullied fame. Throughout Europe his character is known, and respected. In the limits of his own land he is counted if not the first, one of the first and most honoured of her sons and in his own state he is regarded with pride and affection.

Judge Porter pressed me to accompany him to Nashville in Tennessee, where he was going to see his brother. I had not time for that, but I accompanied him as far as Harrodsburgh Springs. As he travelled in his own carriage, we got on slowly, but the drive was through a beautiful country, and I had a pleasant companion whose conversation made the way seem short. He has read extensively, possesses a great fund of general information and, to my surprise, is intimately acquainted with the lighter modern literature.

We parted at the Springs. There is a square of cottages built at these Springs, capable of accommodating four or five hundred people, large room to eat in, grounds laid out without the slightest pretension to taste, stupid hole. The gentlemen pass their time smoking, dram drinking, playing cards and nine pins. Sometimes you may see a knot of them seated with their heels higher than their heads, talking of their bargains and their profits and *reckoning*, *expecting* and *guessing* at a great rate. The ladies, Lord help them, I don't know what they do. I suppose, drink the water, take their tea, walk in the Piazza, and criticize their neighbours' dresses.

Henry overtook me at the Springs; went next day to Shakers-town, stayed there two days. Three hundred in the community, industrious, worthy people — have comical notions though — settled there about twenty years, during which they have cleared a farm of 2,500 acres. Good farmers, raise a great many fine cattle for which they get very high prices. Those who have trades work at them. Dress and language same as the

Quakers. Principal point of belief is that our Saviour was a second time revealed in Anna Lee, and that the Millenium has commenced. They do not marry, not thinking it lawful for Christians. Mr. Clay had given me a letter to the Principal. He was not there, but an old Brother named Hopewell Maynell to whom I gave the letter, begging him to read it, and attend to the request it contained. Answered yea, I will, verily I will. He was a worthy old man, and was very kind to me in his own simple way. He lent me the books to read containing a summary of their views, and a copious account of many miracles that Mother (as they call Mistress Anna Lee) had performed. These miracles attested to by a cloud of witnesses, many of whom were alive at the time the book was published.

We were present one Sunday at the performance of their religious ceremonies. The men took their seats at one side of the room, and the women at the other. At a signal from one of the elders, they rose and rattled off a hymn to a very lively tune, something resembling " Paddy O'Rafferty." The singing was accompanied by a springing on the foot, and a swaying of the body to and fro. After the hymn was concluded, one of the brethren delivered a short address, and a very rigmarole discourse it was. The speaker laboured under a great loss, both for words and ideas, and whenever he came to fault he gave a peculiar nasal twang something like the sound that a beginner first extracts from a French horn. When the exhortation was concluded, they sang another hymn the burthen of which was

" Nay, nay, nay, nay, nay, nay, nay
The old constitution still says nay."

They then removed the benches to the ends of the room, and having thus cleared the decks for action, they formed in line four or five deep, with their faces to the Wall. The men had their coats off, the women were dressed in white, pale, miserable looking articles these women were, with their ghastly countenances, long white robes and close caps. They seemed like corpses risen from the grave with the dead clothes round them, to take part in some unearthly rites.

One of the elders gave a preliminary drone, and then burst out into a lively howl. Immediately the party joined in full cry, dancing forward and backward. As the music grew livelier the dancing grew fast and furious. They hopped and flung and whirled round, and clapped their hands, and yelled like Furies. They were in an awful state of excitement. I marked them closely, and in almost every eye I saw the glare of fanaticism kindled. It was most amusing to see the grim looking stiff rumped old shakers capering about so briskly, and yet with such demure countenances. I would not wish to see again such an exhibition of the absurdities to which fanaticism can lead men.

The pranks of the human mind are quite unaccountable. They cannot be happy, it is impossible, they have voluntarily flung aside all those human sympathies and affections that sweeten life. They have nothing to interest their hearts and feelings, nothing to engage them but the asceticism of a fanatical creed.

It is the illusions of life that render it endurable. It is the deceptive hopes still flitting before us that keep the heart from sinking. He for whom the world has lost its illusions, he who has learned to view life as it is in its cold, dull reality, must feel a chilling sickening indifference at heart, and either lie down and die of the fatal knowledge, or drag on a weary and miserable existence.

The country where the Shakers have made their location is very picturesque. From my window at the top of the house I had a fine view every morning of the green pastures of the Brotherhood, in rolling hill and dell and sweeping upland while the prospect was bounded on every side by the distant forest.

The banks of the river at this place are most romantic; four or five hundred feet high. The stream is walled in by steep rocks that are festooned with trees growing from every crevice and crowned on the summit by pines, on whose lofty branches the sunbeams break but seldom penetrate the dark glen below.

August 15th. Returned to Lexington.

From what I have seen of the climate of America, I am convinced that it is not healthy. The fierce extremes of heat and cold that are experienced, and the sudden changes of temperature (the thermometer varying sometimes twenty or thirty degrees in one day) must be very trying on the constitution. There is none of that equality of temperature which is so favourable to health.

The appearance of the people, particularly those who dwell to the Eastward of the Alleghanies, proves that the climate is unhealthy. The men are almost invariably bad complexioned, lathy, wall sided, round shouldered fellows, with a *tout ensemble* adequately described by no other term than Yankey-ishness. I don't suppose that a set of such looking men could be met with anywhere else than America. The women are generally thin and pale faced, with flat ricketty figures.

I have now seen much of Kentucky and have been greatly struck with its beauty and fertility. It is indeed a glorious country. What a pity that it should be under the curse of slavery! There is little prospect of this question being soon disposed of. It is one of the most difficult and delicate questions, which is agitated in the United States and one which perhaps more than any other, threatens the peace and integrity of the Union. It has already produced serious dissensions and heart burnings between the Northern and Southern States, and will, if not timely legislated, be productive of great evil.

The difficulties that attend this question are increasing every day. Yet those who are most interested in the adjustment of it one way or other, seem afraid to look at it in the face and unprepared to adopt any measures to obviate the dangers which it confessedly threatens.

The Northern and Eastern States, which are free from the curse of slavery, have raised a great outcry about abolition. Societies have been formed, meetings held, pamphlets published, and emissaries employed for the purpose of awakening the public mind and exciting a feeling against the slaveholders in the South. The exertions of the abolitionists have unfortunately been too often characterised by mistaken zeal and inflammatory appeals which have had the effect of disgusting the moderate men of both parties and of retarding a calm unimpassioned discussion of the subject.

The Southern, on the other hand, denounce the interference of the Northerns as officious, meddling and resent it as an attempted infringement on their " vested rights." They permit no discussion of the subject and even go so far as to inflict the pains and penalties of lynch law on any one who has the temerity to preach the doctrine of abolition in their borders.

While passion and prejudice so prevail on both sides, it is idle to expect a satisfactory adjustment of the question, and while matters remain as they at present are, the Southern States are hourly exposed to all the horrors of a servile war. It is really fearful to contemplate what may yet occur, not merely what *may* occur, but what in all probability *will* occur. The slave population in number far exceeds the whites. Then there are tribes of hostile Indians on the frontiers eager to embrace any opportunity for retaliating the wrongs they have suffered, and who can tell how soon a slight cause may occur to stir up this inflammable mass, and raise a storm which will sweep the country with frightful desolation. Such in all probability will be the result unless wise measures be taken to avert the evil. So long as the slave question is undisposed of, the Southern States will be the weak point where a foreign enemy may inflict a serious, if not fatal, wound on the Union.

If America had gone to war with France, and the latter power had landed a force in Florida or Louisiana, and then armed the slaves and called to their assistance the Indians, who were then as they are now at war with the United States, what would have been the result? What chance would the white population of the Southern States, scattered thinly over a great extent of country, have had against at the same time, a foreign enemy, their own slaves in revolt, and an active and relentless Indian foe.

According to the Federal Constitution each state has the sole regulation of its domestic concern. As Congress then cannot interfere, the settlement of the question rests entirely with the slave holding states and they, so far from being disposed to legislate on the matter, scout the very consideration of it and declare that they will resist to the death, any interference or any change in the system. This is strange language and inconsistent conduct on the part of men who boast of their country as being peculiarly the Land of Liberty, and who refer with pride to their Declaration of Independence, in which it is asserted that all mankind are born equal. With what face can they talk of the equality of human rights, they who are traffickers in human flesh?

But, though slavery cannot be defended in any country, and least of all in America, it may to a certain degree be palliated. The people of the Southern States may say, we did not institute slavery. We, but take matters as we found them. From the nature of the climate the produce of our country cannot be raised by white labour.

If you emancipate our slaves you deprive us of the property which we have purchased, you render our plantations worthless. You make us and our children beggars, and you turn loose on us an idle and ignorant population, who will not work unless compelled and many of whom will resort to pillage for support, and care should be taken, lest in the attempt to achieve a speculative good, positive evil might be inflicted. These considerations are not without weight. They show what difficulties attend a question and what extreme caution and circumspection will be required in effecting any change. There is no doubt that a total, immediate, and unconditional emancipation of the slaves would be destructive of the Southern States. And I am convinced that instead of benefitting the slaves, it would inflict on them positive injury. Any change that may be effected should be cautious and gradual. Men who have been bred and born in slavery cannot at once assume the attitude and spirit of freemen.

Slavery in itself is an evil of great magnitude, a system of abomination which no Christian country should suffer and it draws with it a train of the most pernicious consequences. The slaves are not the only victims to this system. The masters themselves suffer, their minds and hearts and habits are completely the possession of an almost irresponsible power. Their morals are contaminated, their energies are never called into action, their characters and feelings are perverted by the circumstances in which they are placed. In the Southern States, society is rotten to the core. It is the same in all slaveholding countries.

Though I hate and detest slavery and hate it still more intensely in a country where I have heard such a prating about equality, yet I must do the slaveholders the justice to say that the grossest mis-statements have gone abroad respecting the treatment the Negroes receive. There are no doubt instances of cruel oppression but as far as I have seen or could learn the general condition of the slaves is comfortable, immeasurably more so than that of the Irish peasantry. They are well fed, well clothed, well lodged; in sickness they are comfortably nursed, and in old age comfortably provided for, and in many cases, there is the most kind and cordial feeling existing between them and their masters. Still slavery is a curse and a blot on the country and should be removed, not so much for the sake of the Negroes as of the Whites.

19th. Took leave of my friends in Frankfort and started by the stage for Louisville. Company in the coach—the Sheriff of the County, a cadaverous looking gentleman who bore a strong resemblance to a Turkey Buzzard—two or three substantial farmers—a doctor, whose plump round about appearance, showed that he took few of his own prescriptions—and the doctor's lady, a very angular piece of mortality, tightly laced up in a faded black silk gown. She also wore a tawdry white bonnet, not very clean and bedecked with a profusion of artificial flowers. Her features were sharp and vixen looking, her bright little black eyes were continually glancing about as if in search of something, her thin prim lips looked as if they had been stuped in a composition of starch and vinegar and to complete her charms her voice sounded like the creaking of a door. It was a very disagreeable voice and I have no doubt the doctor also thought so from the involuntary start he gave whenever its notes fell upon his ears.

After some conversation about the roads, the weather and the crops one of the gentlemen in the usual inquisition style of Americans addressed me. " I reckon Sir, you're not from this section of the country?" I replied in the negative. " You're from the South I expect?" " I am an Irishman." " Hum, ha, from Ireland," said the doctor. " Oh, my," said the lady. " You speak English tolerably plain," pursued my first querist. " Oh, sir," said I, " I have been in the country six months, and have paid much attention to the language. I don't despair of mastering it yet." " Well, stranger," said he, in an encouraging tone, " when you have been among us a year or two, you will speak it nearly as well as ourselves."

They asked me many questions about Ireland, of which they had very curious ideas. The lady chimed in and displayed great fluency of speech. She was a learned lady, moreover, and seemed to pride herself on the fund of general information which she possessed. She took pity on my ignorance and enlightened me on many points. Among other things, I learned from her that Holland is the chief town of Germany. The doctor ventured at times to put in a word: he deplored the bad prospects of the medical men this season, declaring with a melancholy shake of his head that he never knew that part of the country so healthy.

21st. Started with three companions in the stage for Vincennes. Terrible roads, to me they appeared in some places quite impracticable for any carriage to pass, however, we got along without accident. Awful jolting, corduroy roads, very ingenious contrivances for dislocating people's bones. Driver remarked: "Tarnation rough roads, but we streak along pretty smart, I reckon."

If Job had been jolted for a hundred miles over corduroy roads his patience would have been fairly shaken out of him. Stopped the first night at a log house, the day had been intensely warm, the night was cold and frosty. We all slept huddled together in one room, started next morning at three o'clock, arrived at Vincennes in the evening. From Louisville to Vincennes, with the exception of a few clearings and hamlets, the road runs through a continued forest. The country is rolling, consisting of a succession of ridges and vallies, the latter contain very rich land.

Vincennes is an old French settlement, and contains between two and three thousand inhabitants. It is built on the Wabash, in a plain of considerable extent. In winter the low lands, for the distance of nine miles round, are flooded.

Common labourers' wages in Indiana: from twelve to fourteen dollars a month *with board*—a blacksmith can make four dollars a day—mechanics of all kinds in this country would do remarkably well.

Standing in the bar room of the tavern today, I heard a man

thus inviting an acquaintance to take a dram. " Major we're about *liquorizing*, do you feel a notion?" " Well then," replied the major, " I do feel almighty drouthy, there's pretty considerable of a sun today, I expect," and so they took their grog.

24th. Went to Terre Haute — passed over a few small prairies, of four or five miles in circumference. Some of them are partially cultivated and yield fine crops of Indian corn. After travelling for hours through the dense forest, it is delightful to see one of these sunny meadows opening on the river, with its tall grass and bright wild flowers.

Terre Haute seated on the Wabash — small village — situation pretty.

Taverns in the Western County do not afford particularly good accommodation. There are generally a dozen or more beds in each room. I have seen as many as thirty seated along the floor, and the guests pig together two and three in a bed. Hitherto, I have insisted on having a bed to myself, in which my hosts have thought me very unreasonable. In these dormitories, if one is excessively tired and has a very thick hide, one may contrive to sleep. But if your skin is too tender to resist the attacks of the swarms of mosquitoes, bugs, and other vermin, you must just lie awake as patiently as you can, listening to the snorting and snoring of the animals around you. You will be ready to jump up as soon as daylight appears, and then as basons and jugs are luxuries unknown in this part of the country, you have to go out and perform your toilet at the pump.

The village politicians assemble every evening under the piazza of the tavern, kick their heels together, swing themselves on their chairs, and discuss the news of the day. Yesterday evening a knot of them was assembled as usual. After talking on various subjects one of them produced an advertisement of a lot of land he wished to sell. In this paper occurred the word " breadth," which the writer spelled *breath*. " Well," said one of the company, " I reckon there's no such word in the English language as that there word *breath*." " I say there is," answered the writer of the piece, nettled at his " caliology " being corrected. " I say, there's not," said the other. " I expect you're a liar."—"I expect you're a tarnation liar."

Whereupon the two gentlemen showed hostile intentions and I thought I should soon have an opportunity of witnessing a gouging or dirking scene, but the difference was composed by the mediation of the others, and after some debate it was decided that the word was breadth. Well then, said one if the word is breadth, how is it spelled. Here was a fresh cause of contention one spelled it *bregth*—another *bredh*—the squire was appealed to as a man in authority. " *Bredth*," said he with a dictatorial air, " bredth, of course." The doctor happened to be coming along. " Oh!" cries one, " here's the doctor, he'll spell it as slick off as if he had the dictionary in his hand. Doctor how do you spell the word?" The doctor spelled it correctly, but they were not satisfied, and it is still a disputed point in Terre Haute how the word should be spelled.

In discussing the merits of the different candidates for the Presidency, I have heard it objected to Mr. Van Buren that he drives an *English* carriage. Indeed in many of the newspapers this is brought forward as a serious charge, and it has been contradicted with great gravity by Mr. Van Buren's organs.

Left Terre Haute, and after a long journey through the woods, reached a little hamlet called Covington. Here I have taken up my quarters for some days, having a letter from Mr. C. to Mr. H., a member of Congress, who resides here. I went to call upon him. I was shown to a small frame house, at the door of which sat a rather good looking young woman, nursing a squalling child. Mr. H. was not in but she invited me to sit down, saying that he would be back in a few minutes. The room was very small, but neatly and cleanly furnished, a couple of rifles, powder horns and shot pouches graced the walls, and on a shelf was a small collection of standard works from which I augured well of the taste of the proprietor. The apartment seemed to fulfil all the purposes of an eating, sleeping and drawing room. Through an open window, I saw the kitchen which was a very rudely constructed log hut at the rear of the house — this was the residence of a Western legislator.

In the course of conversation, I discovered that the lady was Mrs. H., that she looked upon her husband as the wisest, bravest, best of mortal men. A very proper feeling by the way, and one which every good wife should have for her mate. Having waited for some time, and Mr. H. not appearing, she sent a boy with me to look for him. I soon discovered the object of my search. I told him I was the bearer of an introductory letter to him from Mr. C. He read it, shook hands with me and said it would give him great pleasure to shew me every attention in his power.

The Honorable Member had not been very attentive to his toilet that morning, he was unwashed, unshaved, unclean shirted. He apologised for his appearance, saying that he never dressed on Sunday as it was a day of rest. He is a most enthusiastic sportsman and spends his days in the woods. He says his feelings are similar to those of Hawkeye in the novel, it goes to his heart to see a tree cut down. He talks of soon resigning his seat in Congress as his duties detain him so many months of the year in Washington, where he feels like a fish out of water. He says that always on his return home, when he gets to the top of Laurel Mountain, the point of the Alleghanies, from which the Western Country is first seen, his eyes fill with tears of joy.

Covington is on the verge of the forest. In front is the Wabash, and on the opposite side is a broad prairie. The country around is beautiful.

Society here is quite in its infancy, a system of the most

perfect equality prevails. Next to the Member, the man of greatest importance is the blacksmith. He is considered a person of great prowess, having killed several Indians in his time. He delivers his opinions with great emphasis and in a tone of authority that admits of no contradiction.

This is what they call ague weather. The days are excessively warm and the nights cold, so much so that we are obliged to burn fires. The neighbours are in the habit of gathering round the tavern fire, passing sentence on public men, and discussing weighty political questions with great glibness.

I have been exploring the country here, rambling through the woods and over the prairies, vainly endeavouring to encounter a wolf, but though they are very numerous I have seen none yet. They are extremely wary and sagacious, and very difficult of access. At night they fill the woods with their melancholy howling.

Had a narrow escape from a falling tree — it fell close to me with a thundering crash. Trees that have been girdled and are decayed about the root, tumble down whenever it blows fresh. During a windy day, it is very unsafe to walk near these girdled trees.

Fort El Morro, Havana

Posada de la Bella Europa, Havana

Cocina de Posada de la Bella Europa

Una Volante, Havana

Una Casa, Havana

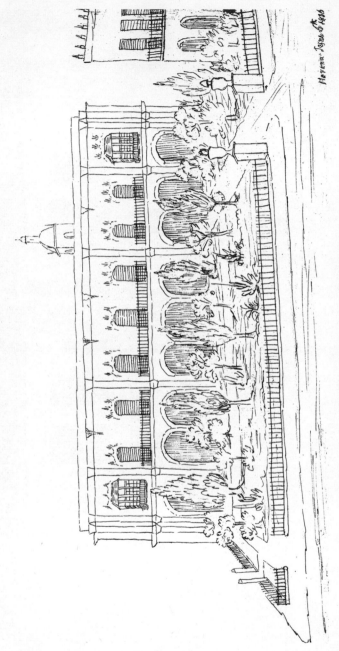

Plaza del Gobernador, Havana

Iglesia de San Pedro, Havana

Iglesia de San Francisco, Havana

EL CATEDRAL

Havana 21 May, 1856

El Catédral, Havana

Havana. Novr. 21. 1836

Uno Convento, Havana

Convento de San Augustino, Havana

Regla outside of Havana

Plaza de Toros, Regla

Spanish Cathedral, New Orleans

New Orleans Feb. 6. 1856

Woodman's Hut on the Mississippi River

Bridge on the Kentucky River

View along the Kentucky River

September 1836

It is the first of September, a warm, sunny day. Have had a long walk through the woods, and am now seated on a log, beneath the shade of a broad tree. The river flows at my feet, the Wabash, as the Indians call it, which means the beautiful river, and beautiful it is, with its clear winding stream and thickly wooded banks. On the other side of the river stretches far away the level prairie, and behind me lies the dark and solemn forest. It is a lonely and a lovely scene, the innovating hand of man has left no traces here. The old woods present the same appearance they did ages ago, and the sward of the prairie has never been broken by the plough. The combination of wood and water, thicket and glade, sunshine and shadow, form a landscape whose charms are felt, but cannot be described by me.

I have been sitting here for some time but not without company. A squirrel is playing itself on the branches of a neighbouring tree, now and then it stops its antics and looks enquiringly at me as if it wondered what I was about. On a sand bed on the other side of the river a heron is standing with one leg drawn up and its head depressed with an air of grave and solemn abstraction, like a lonely hermit musing on the vanity of life. Kingfishers pass and repass on rapid wing, their bright plumage gleaming in the sunshine like gold. The jay utters its harsh discordant notes, like a shrewish wife scolding her husband. The turtle lifts its head out of water and after reconnoitring the neighbourhood, lays itself on a log to enjoy the warmth of the sun, while at times the lordly eagle, from his airy height wakens the echoes with his scream, at the sound of which the heron starts from its contemplative mood, and casts a hasty and alarmed look upwards, the turtle drops with a splash into the water, and the impudent jay, as if the royal bird would condescend to stoop at so mean a quarry, ceases its chattering, and hides itself among thick leaves. It is the first of September, Summer has passed and winter will soon be come. Time with his swift and silent footfalls, the grey traveller whose goal is eternity. Time, the destroyer hurries along " leaving his mark upon every brow, and his shadow upon every heart." Again this time next year, if I be alive, instead of wandering through the forest with the free wind of Heaven on my brow, and the rushing of streams, and the glad voice of wild birds in my ear, I shall be seated perhaps among the men of the quirk, the quibble, and the lie, listening to the details of perjury and fraud—faugh—

Oh! for a tongue to curse the bugs, they murder sleep. Prairie wolves sometimes come into the village. One day last Winter, in open daylight, a wolf entered the hamlet and boldly walked into a house where he was killed after a desperate battle.

Rattlesnakes—great quantity of them here—780 of them killed in one day. Mistake to suppose that they always spring their rattle as a warning note, they generally strike and rattle simultaneously. Pigs kill them without danger. The thickness of hide and depth of lard prevent the serpent's fangs entering the veins. Deer kill snakes by leaping on them. Rattlesnakes have a great antipathy against the leaves of the White Ash. If they are touched with a branch of this tree, they writhe and twist themselves apparently in great agony.

Yesterday a Yankee Pedlar drove up to the door in a light one-horse wagon, laden with an assortment of all kinds of notions he dismounted, came into the house with a case under his arm, and addressing the landlord, briskly said, " Well captain, how do you do?" " Keeping just as common," was the answer. " Can I make a trade with you today?" " Don't want anything," said my host buttoning his breeches' pockets with a resolute air. The pedlar proceeded to unstrap his box.

" Don't want anything, I tell you," repeated the landlord stiffly. The pedlar looked up and his eye caught a thong of leather which Obadiah used instead of a watch chain. " Now I declare captain I'm 'stonished to see a gentleman of your 'spectability wear such an ungenteel thing as that bit of leather to your time of day. It's fit for nothing but to hang a dog with. *My* missus wouldn't let me wear sich a thing, not for the universe," and he set to abusing it at such a rate, that my host at last seemed quite ashamed of having such an appendage to his watch. " Come, now, major," said the Yankee in an insinuating tone, " I warrant you'll be running for member of the legislation some of these days, and it wouldn't do at all to go round the 'lectors with such a thing as that. Now, here's a chain," said he dangling before Obid's eyes an immense steel chain with links that might have served for a cable, " here's an elegant chain, the very ditto of the one the President himself wears and I'll let you have it for a trifle."

Now Obid, from the vituperation that had been lavished on the leather article, was heartily ashamed of it, and his eyes were dazzled by the bright looking ware of the pedlar. I saw that his resolution was giving way when the door opened and in came the landlady with her two gawky daughters trooping after her. I foresaw that the ladies and the pedlar would carry the day. Obid's faint remonstrance was overruled, and in a few minutes the contents of several cases and packages were strewed about to the great admiration of the ladies. " Now, Marm," said the pedlar to the landlady, " I will show you some goods in this here package, that's a sight to look at. Look here, Marm," said he, exhibiting a gown piece, " did you ever lay eyes on such a pattern as that? It's dear, Marm, it's dear, but I know you'll not regard the price, and if you and your sisters each take a piece, I'll make them as low as possible."

" Well I vow, that's good, them ere gals is my darters." The
pedlar dropped his yardstick with a look of well feigned astonishment, " Your darters, Marm, well upon my say so, you
'stonish me, well, well. You must have married considerably
early, but the gals is pretty gals, and it's easy seen who they
took their beauty from, no offence to you, Sir. Howsomdever,
if so be as how you were dressed in one of these here pieces,
there are few girls in the State, would take the shine out of
you at a camp meeting." Now it required unparalleled impudence to stand up and make such a complimentary speech to
a withered old vixen like my landlady, however she swallowed
the flattery, gross as it was, crying out with a blush of gratified
vanity, " Oh, you tarnal critter." The girls giggled, and my host
in a quiet tone ejaculated, " Oh Lord ! "

" Lawkes, Sister," said Miss Prudence Brown, " what dread-
ful nice handkerchers I declare." " I'll have one of the blue
ones," said one. " And I'll have one of the pink ones," said the
other. Then came the bargaining and hizzling. The " much too
dear " of the landlady and the " I couldn't take it, I assure
you " of the pedlar. At last the Yankee settled the dispute by
saying, " I assure you on the honour of a gentleman, Marm,
it's the lowest possible price, lowest price indeed, Marm, I do
not deal like other merchants. My motto is low prices and
quick sales, that's the way I do business."

Mrs. B., having made an additional purchase of a breastpin
for her man to make him look 'spectable, said, " Now Obid,
dear, pay the gent." Obid knew perfectly well that this was
tantamount to saying, ' Go and do it directly,' so he went to
his money drawer with a look of desperate resignation, and
paid the pedlar to the tune of twenty or thirty dollars. However before he took his departure, he asked for a " leetle drop
of brandy just to keep the tarnation ague out of my stomach."
Having tossed off his grog in a twinkling, he leaped into his
wagon, cracked his whip, and drove off to practise on some

more of the natives. "Well," said mine host, after he was fairly gone, " if that ere Yankee Pedlar, or any other Yankee Pedlar, sets foot again in my house I'll be — " and he muttered something in his throat, which sounded very like an oath. " Come, Mr. Brown," said his wife, "don't be imperint; I'll have none of your imperince. Was it for this, I married you, answer me that. I'm ashamed of you, I am, and before the foreign gentleman too." Obid sat down silent and ashamed at the rebuke of his better half.

Took leave of my friends at Covington and set off for Lafayette. Passed over some beautiful prairies, among others, the Shawnee and Weal Prairies. In one of these I saw a circular line of mounds, enclosing a space of about a mile in circumference. These mounds, I was informed, are old Indian burying grounds. Lafayette, small place, landlord an Irishman. As he was whisking the dust off my coat after I arrived : " Well," said he, " that's the very moral of a coat that Mr. McDermott of Ballyduff used to wear. I'll be bound it was made in New York at least." " It was made in the old country," said I. " In the ould country," said he, " then it's an Irishman you are." " To be sure I am," I replied. " You're heartily welcome to my house and the best in it is at your service. Sure whenever I saw you stepping in the door, I knew you were not an American anyhow."

He went on to tell me that he had been about fifteen years in the country, commenced as driver of a wagon, then of a stage, came to Lafayette when that Settlement was formed a few years before. Engaged in the tavern as barkeeper, " though it's little I knew of it," said he, and afterwards became land- lord himself and according to his account was making a *power* of money. " But I'm cruel lonely," continued he. " I have neither wife nor chick nor child, nor a sowl to care about me. If I had time I would go home and marry a decent Irish girl. I believe they make the best wives after all." I asked him how he liked the country. "Why then, the country's a good country and a fine place for a man that's industrious, no man need be in want who will work, but Sir," said he dropping his voice, "are you a Catholic?"

I gave him a nod and left him to interpret it as he pleased, he took it affirmatively and proceeded. " Well then, Sir, there's no religion in this country at all, at all, Divil a taste I believe in my sowl, there's not a man goes to confession from one end of the year to the other, they're worse than the Indians, so they are." After condoling with him on the want of proper religious feeling. I requested he would give me a clean bed to sleep in. " To be sure, to be sure, the best accommodation in the house is at your service, and, moreover, I'll put you in a room where only two more are to sleep." And he did put me in a room where only two others lay, but as to sleeping, that was quite out of the question, such swarms of bugs attacked us, that it was quite impossible to close an eye.

I heard my fellow-lodgers tossing and tumbling and groaning and imprecating all kinds of curses on the bugs. I was ready to get up and dance through the room with sheer rage. At last, one calls out, " I say, stranger, do you feel anything?" " To be sure I do," said I. " Well I guess these tarnation bugs will catawampously chaw me up before morning." There was nothing for it but patience, then we lay till daybreak suffering unutterable tortures.

Next morning continued my journey. Passed over the battle ground of Tippecanoe. It is a narrow strip of land enclosed on three sides by a marsh. Indian force composed of the Pottowatomies, Miakies and Ottoways. The battle was fought in the absence of the great chief, Tecumseh, who was in Arkansas raising warriors. The Indians crossed the swamp and attacked Harrison's army before day break. The fight was desperate — several who were in the battle told me they thought if Tecumseh had been present, the Americans would have been

beaten. His brother the Prophet, sat on a log during the conflict and kept chanting a war song. As soon as victory decided
for the Whites, he disappeared and has never since been
heard of.

Got to Logansford, a few scattered wooden houses on the
Indian frontier.

Had a letter for General Tipton. Walked about a mile along
the bank of the river to his house which was prettily situated
in a little plot embosomed with woods. Not finding him at
home returned to Logansford. When I met him and delivered
my letter—while he was reading it, I took a survey of him.
He was a spare, square built, muscular man. His features were
hard, but set off by a keen, shrewd looking grey eye, and an
expression about the brow and a peculiar set of the mouth
which plainly indicated decision of character. He read the
letter, turned it over, examined it on every side, looked at me
in silence, and then down at his own feet. At last he opened
his mouth and spake : " Could you make it convenient to pass
this evening at my house?" " I dare say I might," said I. " Very
well, Sir, good morning."

Mr. H. had prepared me for his manner. Like most of the old
backwoodsmen I have met, he was very sparing of his words,
and slow and grave in his demeanour. This is generally the
effect of a life spent in the solitude of Nature.

General T. was one of the earliest settlers. He came there
with nothing but his rifle, battled it for years against the
Indians, and is now the greatest proprietor in the State, and
is one of its representatives in the U.S. Senate.

I went to his place in the evening in company with a jolly
faced old gentleman whom I overtook on the road, and who
was introduced to me as Judge P. The evening threatened to
pass off stiffly enough till I asked our host some questions
about the battle of Tippecanoe, at which I knew he had made
a figure. I saw I had gained his heart by the interest I took in

the subject, his eye brightened, he drew his chair closer to mine, and began and fought his battle over again. The puzzle-pated old judge chimed in too. He, when a youth, had been a captive among the Indians, of whose habits and manners he gave me an interesting account. When I rose to come away, the general cordially pressed me to take up my abode at his house, a species of hospitality very rare in America.

I have just returned from a most interesting excursion among the Indians, the wild tribes of the prairies and the far forests, whose virtues and views are still their own, uncorrupted and unalloyed by mixture with the whites. On leaving home for America, it was my firm intention to see the Indians in their native woods and I was determined to gratify my wish at all hazards.

Having remained a day or two at a border settlement to get all necessary information, I started early one fine morning, well mounted, and prepared, and took my lonely path into the forest, with my heart high and my spirits roused and excited at the thought of the new scenes I was about to witness, any adventures, or perhaps dangers, which I might have to encounter.

There is no mode of travelling so delightful as on horseback, provided your horse be good, but if he is a dull heavy-headed brute, it is utter vexation of spirit, and a grievous trial of one's patience. My steed, however, was one of the right sort, strong limbed, spirited and hardy. I never felt more elation of spirit than when I found myself in the depth of the gloomy forest. My nerves in good tone, and my heart raised to that pitch when it is capable of reaping enjoyment from every thing.

People may talk as they will about the charms of human society ; it is very charming no doubt, but there is a heart felt *delight*, an unutterable pleasure in being alone, in certain circumstances. Zimmerman has discoursed very learnedly about this, but I am not sure that he ever experienced the passion in its fullest extent, nor do I think he ever had any adequate idea of what it really is. What is solitude in a comfortable country mansion with a retinue of well ordered servants to attend you, or even in a mountain hermitage within a few leagues of a populous town, and in the midst of a civilized and well ordered country? What is that to being alone in the wild, and gloomy, and almost boundless forests of the New World, when almost every tree and shrub is strange to you, when every bird whose voice breaks the stillness is unknown to you, when you are not only far removed from the pale of civilization, but when thousands of miles of angry sea roll between you and your native land? To be in such a situation, is to feel, according as the person's mind is constituted, either the horrors, or the charms, of solitude.

It was a most lovely day. The sky was blue and clear without even a fleecy cloud to dim its brightness. The heat was such as we never experience in Ireland, even in the hottest of the dog days. All Nature seemed basking in the sunshine, not a leaf was stirring and not a sound was to be heard in the forest, but at times a woodpecker hammering at a decayed tree. Having struck a trail along the bank of a river I followed it according to directions I had received and after a long and wearisome journey found the hut of the woodman to whom I had an order from the Indian agent to act as my interpreter. This person was half French and half Indian, but spoke English tolerably well.

His dress was a combination of the white man's and the Indian's. He wore a hunting shirt, leggings and mocassins, and a nondescript kind of head dress, which was neither hat nor cap; a belt of undressed deer skin passing over his shoulder sustained a bullet pouch, and another of a similar kind round his waist held a long knife and a tomahawk. His complexion was a dirty yellow, a few straggling dark hairs graced his cheeks and chin, his eyes were black and deep set and had the sinister expression of a wolf's. Altogether his appearance was such as would not have induced me to put much faith in him, but when I scanned his make, I was satisfied that if anything should occur to bring us to *grips*, I should not be second best, unless he were particularly dexterous in the use of his knife. Feeling it would be bad policy to evince any distrust I entered into familiar conversation, gave him accounts of the wonders of the cities of Europe at which he listened with gaping astonishment, and told me in return many of his adventures and perils in the woods. We became tolerably good friends.

Next morning, accompanied by my host, I set off into the bowels of the land, and after many incidents by " flood and fell " arrived safely at the lodge of the Grand Pottowatomie Chief, who in sullen state lived a considerable distance apart from his tribe. We found him seated in his wigwam with several Indians. The interpreter made known my wishes. I then made a speech expressing myself as well as I could in the metaphorical manner of the Indians. I said that " I had come from the rising Sun over the Great Salt Lake to see my red brothers, that I had heard they were brave warriors and good hunters, and I wished to see how they lived that I might tell the young men of my tribe to take example from the Pottowatomies," and some more nonsense of the same sort.

Above all, I begged him distinctly to understand that I was not a Yankee. The chief replied and as it was the first time I had heard an Indian speak, I was almost startled by the deep guttural intonations of his voice. He went on to say that I spoke good words, that the path was open, and concluded by saying that I was welcome, and that two of his young men would go before me. He then shook hands with me and introduced the other Indians, each on being introduced came slowly forward, grasped my hand tightly and gazed earnestly in my face for a few moments. There was an old gentleman, who, the interpreter told me, was a great warrior. He was a very peculiar looking gentleman, his features were harsh and strongly marked, his brows very projecting and his deep set eyes sparkled like coals of fire. His naked breast was seamed with wounds. He wore a rude necklace, and a very uncouth ornament in his nose.

He walked slowly across the floor with noiseless step, his eyes bent on the ground, and when he came to me he held out his hand and turned up his face to mine with such a keen inquiring expression that I was tempted to laugh outright. I felt my lip twitching, and could scarce restrain myself but stealing a glance towards the interpreter. I saw him regarding me with an angry and warning frown, so I composed my countenance, looked as demure as a cat after stealing cream, took the old warrior's hand and gave it a hearty squeeze. After gazing at me some time longer, he uttered a grunt and walked slowly back to his place. We then sat down in a circle and smoked a pipe deliberately. *Not* the Calumel which I believe is only used on solemn occasions.

" Fire water " was then introduced and passed round in a gourd. We were a very sedate party. I imitated their demeanour as closely as possible and answered the few questions put to me by my " red brothers " with becoming gravity. After remaining there some time, the Indians rode up to the wigwam, these were my promised guides Mamaseehwa and Pokewa, the good warrior and the black wolf, as my interpreter told me, who having given me many directions as to how I was to comport myself, and warning me not to do anything which might give offence, even by looks, took his leave to go off into the wilderness on a hunting excursion. With these two Indians, I took a very wild ride, such as I never had before, and such as, I suppose, I shall never have again. They were very polite but seemed to have very little regard for their own neck or mine either.

" We stayed not for brake, and we stopped not for stone.
We swam many rivers when ford there was none."

But I must describe my guides. Mamaseehwa was rather low, stout made, hawk featured, and had a voice like the growl of a bear. He was a slovenly rider, did not care how he sat, though in whatever position he was, he seemed to be quite at ease and I had proof that he kept his seat so tenaciously that few horses could dismount him. Pokewa was a tall lithe, fine looking young fellow. His features were regular, his eyes well opened, and sparkling, and his mouth, which is rather unusual among the Indians, was small and handsome. He sat his horse firmly and gracefully, and seemed to take pride in displaying his horsemanship by riding at difficulties which a short detour would have avoided.

At one time at a hand gallop, we came to a dark deep river, the bank on our side was steep and rugged, the bank on the other side was also so steep that I thought no horse could get up. As we advanced, I cast my eye up the stream, and saw a place about fifty yards above where there was evidently a ford. I thought Pokewa would take advantage of it, but to my surprise he gave a short scream, urged his horse over the bank, and the next instant I saw man and steed plunging into the water. Mamaseehwa then dashed past me, his horse missed his feet and seemed to tumble headlong. I expected to see them floating separately down the stream but was surprised to behold him and his steed emerging from the plunge and gallantly breasting the current. I had nothing else for it but to do as they did. I knew if I hesitated, they would have looked on me as a cowardly " pale face," so I pressed the hat on my brows, dashed the spurs into my horse, and the next instant found myself half choked, and floundering in the water, but still in the saddle. After swimming across, it was no easy matter to get up the opposing bank. My horse made several attempts; at times he nearly fell back, but by leaning forward on his neck, we at last gained the firm ground.

It was a novel situation and not without a keen sense of

excitement and pleasure to be alone in the wilderness with my savage companions. I felt that one week spent in such scenes " were worth ten years of peaceful life."

Pokewa rode a short distance ahead and seldom spoke. Mama-seehwa kept close beside me and chatted a good deal, though of course what he said was quite unintelligible; however, his gestures were very expressive. We met a warrior painted and plumed. It is scarcely possible to conceive a more savage look-ing object than that wild and warlike figure, yet his air was absolutely imposing. His face and breast were painted red and black, his head was shaved with the exception of the long scalp tuft which was ornamented with a red feather, his belt was furnished with the usual weapons, the tomahawk and knife and in his hand he bore a light bow. He stopped a few minutes and held a short conversation with my guides. Mama-seehwa gave me to understand that he was going on a hostile expedition. He then went on as I gathered from his gestures to tell me an exploit of his own. He concluded by passing his hand significantly round his scalp. Then uttering the war whoop in startling tones that made the forest ring, he urged his horse forward and having galloped some distance in advance, wheeled round and rode back at the same rapid pace. He seemed to be violently excited by his recollections, but soon recovered his cold composure of manner.

During this excursion I visited several villages and at every wigwam where I stopped I was treated so kindly and well with rude, though genuine hospitality of savage life that I formed a most favourable opinion of the natives and I felt more at home and experienced a greater feeling of confidence and security than I ever did among the white inhabitants of the frontier, who, I do verily believe, are far more rude and brutal than the Indians.

The wigwams, in shape some circular, some oblong, are rudely constructed of light poles, covered over with birchen bark. The household furniture is very scanty, a mat or deer skin forms their bed and seats. Their wants are few, and those wants easily supplied. In person they are lightly and actively built and very straight. When not excited they walk along at a slow grave pace, and turn in their toes so much as to give rather an awkward appearance to their gait. They have not that bounding step, which I thought, from their manner of life would have distinguished their movements.

Their faces in general are strongly marked and bear a close resemblance to the Tartar cast of countenance. When seated in silence they have a cold abstracted look as if their thoughts were far away, but when speaking their features become very animated and they use considerable gesture. They wear their hair, in time of peace, long and plaited behind. Some of the women, though not absolutely handsome, had a mild and pleasing expression.

I had an assortment of rings with me, of which I made presents to the *ladies*. When I was putting the rings on their fingers (and pretty little hands they had) they hung down their heads and seemed overcome with bashfulness, with the exception of one squaw. When we entered her wigwam, we found her seated on a bearskin, making a pair of mocassins. Mamaseehwa said a few words to her, upon which she looked at me, smiled and held out her hand with the air of a princess. After shaking hands with her I put four or five rings on her fingers.

She looked alternately at her hands and in my face, laughed merrily and seemed quite delighted with her new ornaments. They are extremely fond of ornaments, value such presents highly and preserve them carefully, so I may hope, through the medium of these rings, long to be remembered in the wigwams of the Pottowatomies as the " pale face " who was once their guest.

One of the villages which I visited was beautifully situated on a green flat, at the base of a wooded hill, having close in its front a pretty winding river, about the width of the Roe. In the vicinity of the village we passed through a grove of wild plum trees. Several Indian girls were gathering the fruit which grew in great abundance, some of them glided out of our way into the thicket, others awaited our approach, turned their eyes on the ground with a look of bashful timidity and made no reply to the few words addressed to them by my guides. As we advanced farther into an open space, we came upon some boys who were busily playing with round flat stones, a game like quoits. These young gentlemen were not encumbered with much dress. Some of the elder ones wore mocassins and leggings, but nothing more. They seemed in high glee, whooping and screaming in ear-piercing notes. As soon as they perceived us they became silent and having honoured me with a broad stare, they resumed their sport.

Some horses were picketted about the village, a number of dogs set up a furious barking at our approach which drew several people to the doors of the wigwams. We stopped at a large circular lodge, where several Indians were standing. My guides held a short conversation with them, after which they all advanced and shook hands with me. Some of them took hold of the bridle, some of the stirrups and some took hold of myself as if to assist me to dismount. One knelt down, and with a band of long grass was proceeding to tie the forelegs of my horse, but from what I had heard of their excitable disposition and of the not unusual occurrence of their throwing their tomahawks at each other's heads, at the conclusion of a feast, I thought it prudent to be on the "qui vive" and to be ready for a start, so I gently tapped my friend on the shoulder and gave him to understand by my gestures that I preferred fastening my horse to the branch of a decayed tree which stood near the wigwam.

At this lodge there was a large party assembled — we had a great feast and the usual speechifying and questions. I flatter

myself that I evinced as much grave decorum as any Sagamon
of the party, though their speeches and questions were of course
beyond my comprehension I endeavoured to satisfy them by
gestures, which if they understood, was more than I did
myself.

But to relate the different incidents or to give you a detailed
account of the different occurrences of this excursion, would
fill a volume and be entirely out of the scope of these hurried
and irregular notes, written sometimes in the saddle, sometimes in my hours of resting, under the shadow of a tree, and
though at present my mind is filled with thoughts of the scenes
through which I have lately passed, and though I am sure I
shall long look back on them with pleasure and interest, yet at
present I have not leisure to describe them as I could wish,
and at a future time, perhaps, I may not have patience to
reduce these notes into order and from these materials to give
an ample and adequate description of the scenes which I
have witnessed.

These Indians are a very roving tribe, they live entirely by
the chase and often wander away in the hunting season many
hundred miles. They are a very warlike tribe and in the last
war particularly distinguished themselves by the gallant stand
they made against the encroachments of the whites on the
Western country.

The Indians are a most interesting people, their heroic
qualities, their tameless nature, their religious opinions so immeasurably superior to those of other savages, their domestic
virtues, their strict integrity and love of justice, their rude
philosophy, their origin, and the vague though in some respects
plausible supposition which would identify them with the lost
tribes of Israel, invest them with a peculiar interest which few
other savage nations possess.

They were at one time numerous along the shores of the
Atlantic Ocean. The arrival of the whites was the date of their

decay. They received the strangers with friendship, but were soon taught by bitter experience to distrust them. By the fraud and tyranny of *Christians* the red men were gradually driven back, their hunting grounds were despoiled, the bones of their fathers were torn up by the white man's plough and they the native sons of the forest were obliged year by year to yield up their heritage to the encroachments of the " pale faces."

By oral tradition, and by a method they have of recording events on their wampum belts, a knowledge of the past is handed down from father to son. I have been told by an American officer who speaks several Indian dialects, and from acting as a commissioner in negotiating treaties has had opportunities of meeting the chiefs and wise men of different tribes, that they deeply feel their decay. To use their own expression, " They are melting away like snow, before the face of the white men. The great Spirit is angry with his red children and the day is not far distant when they shall be driven to the shores of the other sea." A beautiful trait in the Indian character is the undying reverence and affection which they cherish for the memory of their departed friends. They consider it a sacred duty, and one which they never omit at stated times, to visit the graves of their kindred. These spots they consider hallowed and no dangers or difficulties will deter them from the performance of this duty.

One day, riding over a prairie, I was much struck at seeing an Indian seated on the ground beside a little mound. His arms were folded on his bosom, and his head depressed. There he was sitting in lonely and melancholy abstraction, doubtless musing on past scenes, and thinking of the being whose mouldering bones lay near him. It was a good subject for a painting.

The Indians are very successful hunters, they seem peculiarly qualified by nature for this pursuit. They are endowed with amazing powers of endurance and it is almost incredible what toils and hardships they can undergo. Hunger and thirst, and the fierce extremes of heat and cold, they can bear with the most unmoved stoicism. They can live in plenty where a white man would starve. Let them have but a rifle or bow and they will soon supply all their wants.

They are trained to habits of extreme watchfulness and caution. These qualities are of the greatest service to them in war and in the chase. Nothing, even the most minute, escapes their observation, a leaf on the ground broken, ruffled or misplaced, a broken twig arrests their attention, and a short examination enables them to tell the cause.

In green weather, they can trace a bear or deer, or even smaller game with the greatest certainty. They follow the trail as staunchly as bloodhounds, wind themselves like snakes through the thicket, steal up close to their prey, and seldom throw away a charge of powder; every shot tells.

I was for a long time sceptical as to the stories I heard about the extreme accuracy with which Indians could follow the trail of an animal, be it man or beast, till I was shewn the way it was done. In the forest the ground is generally thickly covered with decayed leaves. These retain any moisture which falls, and thus they are impressed for some time with the trace of anything that has passed over them. An ordinary observer, and one unaccustomed to the woods, will never notice this, but by running the eye along the ground, and looking narrowly, one sees an indistinct wavering line. The Indians whose senses are very acute, and whose experience is so great, will follow a trail at full speed without being obliged to stop in order to observe it closely. They are guided not by the individual impressions, but by the general character of the trail.

But I must conclude these hurried sketches of my Indian excursion, altogether I was greatly pleased with it, and I shall long look with interest on the days I spent among the Pottowatomies.

On our return, having reached the bank of a river along

which ran a narrow trail, the guides reined up and dismounted.
I followed their example. After sitting in silence about half an
hour, Mamaseehwa rose, pointed to the sun, to the river and
the trail, and having by such signs given me many directions as
to my route, they shook my hand several times, then leaping
on their horses rode slowly off and left me to pursue my lonely
way. Strange as it may seem, I felt a certain degree of pain
at parting from these Indians.

By the help of the trail, I succeeded, after a long ride, in
finding the hut of the interpreter. I was so hungry that if he
had not soon got me something to eat, I could have devoured
himself, though he would have been an unsavoury morsel.

Once more in the " clearings," and among people of my own
colour. (I suppose I must call them civilized, though, to tell the
truth, they are more rude and unpolished in their manners and
a thousand times less courteous than my Indian hosts.) I have
often had occasion to notice the extreme curiosity of the
Americans but the people here, in that respect, exceed any I
have yet met. Their inquisitiveness is insatiable, they will not
be put off by any evasion or daunted by any surliness, they
return again and again to the charge, and put their imper-
tinent queries with such an earnest air that one cannot at
length help laughing, however, one may at first be disposed
to be angry. Where are you going? Where did you come from?
What's your business? What's your name? Are you married
or single?, are generally the first questions put by a stranger.
I found the best way of baffling them was to answer any inter-
rogation by a similar query.

Started in a wagon (a long open cart) with two companions
for Lake Michigan. Stopped the first night in a log hut in the
woods, two or three travellers joined us, and we all pigged
together on the floor. After supping on the rude cheer, which
the inmates could supply us with, we piled some huge logs on
the hearth and made a fire sufficient to roast an ox, and,

wrapping ourselves up in what covering we could get, lay down before it. In a short time my neighbours gave unequivocal signs of being asleep.

> " Each tuneful nose did lift its voice
> and make strange melody."

Such a concert of all notes and tones and cadences never was heard. It resembled a Dutch concert where every man plays his own tune. Such snorting and grunting and blowing and whistling—snoring in all its branches was exemplified, from the asthmatic snoozling sound that died away with a choking gurgle, in the sleeper's throat, to the full toned grave steady note of the veteran snorer that poured forth a mighty volume of sound with such vigour and emphasis as to make the very window panes crack.

It came on a very wild night. I lay a long time awake listening to the sounds around me and to the rushing of the storm without, mingled with the groaning and the crashing of the trees, while at times in the pauses of the storm, a wolf would lift its voice and utter a long melancholy howl. At last, as the brands were flickering and dying on the hearth, I fell asleep, and despite the bugs, and the manœuvres of a man who lay beside me, and who was afflicted with St. Vitus' dance, slept soundly till day break when I was roused by my fellow-lodgers calling for their *antifogmaticks*.

The sun breaking out bright and joyously dispelled the dark clouds. The birds welcoming the change made the forest resound with their notes, and with every prospect of a fine day we resumed our journey. Two days afterwards I was alone on the shores of Lake Michigan. From the high sand hills which line the beach, I had a splendid view; on one side the smooth blue waters of the lake spread far away, apparently as boundless as ocean, and on the other a dark mass of forest covered the country as far as the eye could reach.

After a long and toilsome ramble through that wild country that lies to the North West of Lake Michigan, I have turned my face again Eastwards, and have now arrived at Chicago where I shall stop two or three days to rest. I have, strange to say, in spite of all the exposure to which I was subject, escaped ague, but the fatigue I have undergone, and some sickness, produced I believe by drinking the bad water of the country, has worn the very flesh off my bones so that I look as gaunt as a famished wolf. When I came here, after having endured so much toil, cold and heat, wet and want of sleep, it was a great luxury to get off my clothes, and turn into a bed, where I slept soundly in spite of the bugs and though the bed linen was none of the cleanest.

When I was shaving this morning, I was at first startled and then moved to laughter at the portrait which a little cracked looking glass presented to me, of a very wasted and embrowned face, covered with a beard of a fortnight's growth. It was not till after I looked at myself some time that I could assure myself of my own identity.

The tavern at which I stop, like all those in the West, is an exceedingly dirty, comfortless place, without the slightest attention or civility on the part of the proprietor. From the manner of the landlord, he appears to think he is actually conferring a favour on his guests by granting anything they require. Though I had made a resolution to take matters as they were, and to put up with " everything but actual aggression or insult," I at last fairly lost my temper with this fellow and, to use the expression of the Methodist preacher, " discharged my soul on him " with great tempestousness. Anger is very improper, to be sure, but still it has sometimes its good effects, like the storm in the natural world, it stirs and purifies the atmosphere and dispels all dark and heavy vapours.

The people in this country seem to think that independence and civility are incompatible. If you go into a settler's house you are received, not with the smiling hearty welcome of an Irish, or the quiet civility of an English yeoman, but with cold and surly demeanour which shews you are looked upon as an unwelcome intruder.

The migration of pigeons has commenced. An immense stream of them has been steadily passing over this place for some hours past, sometimes descending with a sudden swoop almost to the ground. The noise of their wings resembles the rush of a mighty wind. The most distant part of the stream which is visible is like a wreath of vapour rapidly shifting its place, ascending, descending and whirling round. I have been told that when they stop to roost, they cluster in such multitudes on the branches that the mighty forest trees break down beneath their weight.

I had set my heart on visiting Prairie du Chien and having a buffalo hunt, but the season is now so far advanced, and travelling in this remote country is so difficult that I am reluctantly compelled to abandon the intention and turn my face towards Canada. By the lakes it is about 1,300 miles to Toronto and by land about 700 or 800. As time is precious I shall take the latter course — come what may — I must see the Falls of Niagara.

It has been raining incessantly for the last two days. The flat country about this is nearly covered with water. I foresee I shall have an arduous journey across Michigan.

23rd. Started from Chicago in an open wagon in company with two land speculators, and rough-looking " tykes " they were. Travelled on night and day and arrived in Detroit on the night of the 28th.

This has been a very tedious and toilsome journey. Where there *were* roads, they were execrable, such as a European could have no conception of. If a man were to set about describing bad roads and were to draw on the powers of the liveliest imagination, he would fall far short of the realities which I experienced. Sometimes the horses were swimming in water, sometimes floundering through quagmires. At times the wagon was all but upset over stumps of trees. And at some places where a rude civilization had extended and where attempt had been made to form corduroy roads, it went bumping and crashing along in such an awful manner that I did not know whether to wonder more at its timbers not being shaken to pieces, or at *our* bones escaping dislocation.

The second day my two fellow travellers gave up; they declared they could go no further. I pushed on and got to my destination without any accident, though the wagon was upset and smashed to pieces, when we were about forty miles from Detroit. I fortunately was on foot at the time—it was my habit to walk ahead during the day and only take my seat at night.

When I look back on this journey across Michigan, I wonder how I was able to undergo it. My dress was a light shooting one, without any outer coat. The days were blazing hot, the nights very cold, and five days and four nights in succession I travelled on without closing my eyes for an instant. Strange to say, I felt no desire to sleep, and when I arrived at Detroit, so over-stimulated and excited was I that I did not go to bed for a couple of hours, and after I did retire I scarcely slept and was up for breakfast next morning at six o'clock. But in the afternoon I became so drowsy, I went to bed and slept sixteen hours at a stretch.

Michigan is much diversified with prairie and woodland. The soil in general is light, as is evidenced by the nature of the timber that grows on it. Some of the prairies are beautifully interspersed with groves, copses and clumps of trees, that seem almost to have been arranged by the hand of man. I have travelled for a long day through a tract of country that bore all the appearance of a park tastefully laid out and diversified with lawns and groves and forest glades, while here and there a lovely little lake added much to the picturesqueness of the scenery.

In some places I saw good farms and rather comfortable houses, but still the settlers labour under all the disadvantages incident to a new country. The country abounds with game. There are lots of deer, elk, and turkeys, wolves, both the common grey wolf and the prairie wolf, are very numerous and destructive of the farmers' stock. They are very partial to young pigs, and exact their tithe with as much relentlessness as any tithe proctor. One evening, walking along the verge of a prairie, near a settlement, I heard a crashing in the brush wood and presently out dashed a drove of pigs in dire confusion and dismay. In a short time the cause of their consternation appeared. A wolf bolted out of the thicket in full pursuit, slinging himself along in the peculiar canter in which these animals go. The poor pigs seemed dreadfully alarmed at having such an enemy in pursuit. They grunted and *squealed* most vociferously as if calling to heaven and earth for aid. Since the day that the devils entered the drove of swine, such a scrambling, headlong race never was seen—it was devil take the hindmost. At times the last in the race (I suppose instinctively aware of the proximity of its enemy) would utter an agonizing scream upon which the herd would answer with a chorus of grunts and squeaks and set off with, if possible, redoubled speed. It was very laughable to look at, but no joke for the pigs. Pursuer and pursued crossed me at a short distance. I ran up to intercept the wolf, who, when he saw me join the party, slunk off and trotted back to cover, while the hogs scampered away as briskly as ever. I got into the wagon, but we had not driven far when we heard a most outrageous squeaking—the wolf, doubtless, had " bided his time " and caught one of them at last.

The wild turkey is very numerous in this district. It is a very fine bird, larger and with more brilliant plumage than the tame. They go in gangs of a dozen or more, run fast and are hard to be got at. However, once they are flushed and *treed*, a flock will sit quietly till every one is shot, provided the sportsman begins at the lower branch and gradually ascends.

They have a very simple way of taking them in large quantities. They enclose a small plot of ground with a close paling, covered at top, and having an entrance at the foot, by a covered way just large enough to admit a turkey. Some Indian corn is put into the enclosure, and a train of it laid along the entrance. Once the birds find themselves trapped they never attempt to get out by the way they came in, but keep hopping about and leaping up, vainly seeking an outlet at the top.

The first morning, about daybreak, we stopped at a cabin to feed our horses, and saw at the door an emigrant's wagon with two women sitting in it. We asked them what raised them so early. They said the bugs were so annoying, they actually drove them out of the house and forced them to take shelter there. Bugs and fleas are, here, an absolute plague. One of my fellow-travellers told me a story, very amusing from the grave feeling manner in which he related it, of bugs a night or two before, " chawing," as he expressed it, at his ankle till it festered and he thought he should have lost his foot.

Stopped about two o'clock one morning at a log house. Found a party of travellers who had also stopped there to rest and feed their horses. The driver was lying before the fire fast asleep, and snoring with great emphasis. They told us he was a most troublesome brute, that they could not manage him, he had upset them two or three times, putting their necks in most imminent peril, and on arriving there had laid himself down, fallen asleep, and *would* not awake. They kicked him, shouted and halloed in his ear, but still he slept on or affected to sleep. At last one of them, losing all patience, heated the poker and applied it to him. I never saw an application so instantaneously effective; the fellow at once jumped to his feet, uttering a dismal howl like a wolf, and staring stupidly round the party. Then there was the devil to pay — he swore he would thrash them all, threats and menaces were bandied about and we left them in a state of blessed confusion.

During my journey across Michigan, I met numbers of emigrants from the old states on their way to settle in the Western forests. Each emigrant generally had a wagon or two, drawn by oxen. These wagons contained their wives, children, and *rest of their baggage*. The man walked by the side of his team with his rifle over his shoulder, driving before him a load of pigs (animals which are peculiarly adapted for the back woods, where they are always able to procure plenty of grub for themselves, and after getting fat, they make very good grub for the settler and his family). Corned pork is the staple food of the West. When I was there, I could get nothing to eat, morn, noon, and night, but corned pork. I was fed on it till I was ashamed to look a pig in the face.

Many of these emigrants had left comfortable homes in the Eastern States. Bound by no local attachments and impelled by that love of change and restless spirit which distinguishes the Americans, they had abandoned friends and kindred and all the comforts of civilized life to plunge into the wild and dreary forests of the West. Numbers of these emigrants, when they start from home, have no definite point of destination. If you ask one where he is going to, he will likely answer: " Nowhere in particular, but somewhere Westward, I guess." When they arrive at any place which strikes their fancy they make a location, fell some trees, erect a log hut, clear a few acres of ground, and by so doing they acquire what is called a pre-emption claim, so as to entitle them to the first offer when the land comes to be sold. These claims they often sell to speculators and then pack up their traps, shoulder their rifles, and trudge off farther Westward to repeat the same course.

These are the men who are the pioneers of civilization.

After a short stay at Detroit, went down the lake by steamer to Buffalo. This is a very rising town; it has become a place of considerable trade and sprang up rapidly into importance in the last few years. A very enterprising merchant of the town named Rathbun has mainly contributed to its improvements. His speculations were infinitely varied, and numerous, and his schemes gigantic. He engaged in every pursuit in the most extended state. He had upwards of a thousand labourers in his employment; he built mills, hotels, churches, theatres and steamboats. He was, besides, the owner of several lines of stage coaches, and he had two or three entire streets in process of erection. But he went " ahead " rather too fast — a crash came at last. To help him on he had recourse to forgery, and it was discovered that he had committed frauds of this kind to the amount of upwards of two million and a half of dollars. However, I heard everyone expressing great sympathy for him. They said he had unfortunately speculated rather too largely; wholesale forgery they called by the mild name of speculation.

In the house where I stopped there were about two hundred people, all as usual in the most breathless haste. What a Babel of confusion the American hotel is. Such clatter and hurry and scrambling, and the eternal song is about dollars, dollars, dollars!

Throughout the United States, the great equality of condition strikes the stranger. There is no idle class in America, as there is no law of primogeniture and, it being the custom of the country to divide the property of the father equally among all the children, large fortunes are seldom accumulated by *families*. The constant division and subdivision to which property is subject, keeps it pretty equally diffused. This is one of the foundation stones of democracy, and to this, perhaps, may in a certain degree, be ascribed the commercial prosperity of America. The capital of the country, equally diffused, is kept in constant circulation. The energy and enterprise of the people are untrammelled by too much legislation. There are few restrictions on trade, very light taxation, sufficient competition to stimulate to exertion, but not too much to make success difficult, an ample field for industry, and through the system of local government, means afforded to the people to provide promptly anything they may require. With all these advantages added to their own great intelligence and enterprise, it would be strange indeed if the citizens of the United States were not eminently prosperous.

The Americans are essentially a money-making people. They are all engaged in the same headlong race after wealth—in no country is Mammon pursued with greater keenness.

" Their altar is their counter, their Bible is their ledger, their God is their gold "—To do them justice they spend their money freely enough; they are vain, ambitious and ostentatious.

This indiscriminate, incessant pursuit of wealth, this constant struggle in the miry paths of trade, this keeping the mind continually excited on the one point of requisition, the having the daily thoughts and nightly dreams tinged with the hue of gold, must have a very pernicious effect on the national character. An earnest pursuit of trade, the making one's business, whatever it is, one's sole object, has the effect, much more than is supposed, of contracting the mind, and often of soiling the heart.

It is a rare thing to see boys in the United States. The instant a young lad is as tall as the counter, he is togged out in a long skirted coat, put into a store or counting house, and initiated into the mysteries of traffic. He has not had time to receive an education sufficient to enlarge his mind, or elevate his thoughts. From his youth upwards he is conversant with nothing but the practices of his trade, consequently it is not to be wondered at, if his character should be sordid and mercenary, and his conduct often anything but fair and open. In every instance in which I had occasion to purchase anything, I found it quite vain to expect fair dealing. I will say this for the American shopkeeper, that whatever else they may deal in *conscience* is one commodity which they do not possess. This remark may appear too sweeping and unjust. I am convinced it is applicable to the nation at large, though of course there are many many exceptions.

An Englishman in this country, travelling by the steamboats and other public conveyances, mixing with the people at the inns, sitting at the public tables etc., must be surprised at the solecisms in good manners, and often shocked at the abominations he witnesses around him. He sees persons in the garb of gentlemen, guilty of the most flagrant breaches of decorum, and the majority of those with whom he thus mixes are such as no person of any refinement could find the slightest pleasure in associating with, but if he forms his opinion of American *gentlemen* from the specimens he thus meets, his estimate will be very erroneous indeed. The traveller, here, is thrown among a class with whom he seldom comes in contact in other countries, because in other countries the pecuniary means of that class do not permit them to avail themselves of the same conveniences, and comforts of travel, and even if they had the means, the distribution of rank, and the usages of society, would not sanction it.

It has been either a wilful, or involuntary want of attention to this fact, which has led many tourists astray. I have sat at dinner next a person who, as far as the materials of his clothes were concerned, was as well dressed as any person in the room. That person was the servant of a gentleman who was at the same table, and he behaved with as much propriety as most of those who were present. Now if I had taken him as a specimen of an American gentleman (which as a stranger I might have done) and commented on his manners etc. as such, I should have committed a grievous mistake. A gentleman is the same all over the world, the qualities requisite to form the character of a true gentleman are the same in every country : the same high sense of honour, the same integrity of character, the cultivated mind, and the scrupulous regard for the feelings of others. These are the qualities which stamp the possessor (no matter of what climate or colour he may be) a sterling and undisputed gentleman. But I must admit that in America the proportion of such gentlemen is very scarce. Every " man Jack " here calls himself a gentleman, as equality is the boast of the land. One man thinks himself as much entitled as another to dub himself gentleman. If they could assume the character along with the name, it would add immeasurably to the comfort of those who travel among them.

They are fond too of calling themselves a *nation* of *gentlemen* (save the mark) a nation of gentlemen, quotha (I have to lay down my pen to laugh). No, no, Jonathan, stick to what you are ! ! You are a nation of hard working, enterprising, intelligent people, whose independence and prosperity are the work of your own hands. Depend upon it, you will acquire more credit from this character, than from your pretensions to refinement.

The Americans, as a people, are excessively vain. Vain to an extent perfectly ludicrous, and they are so thin skinned, so sensitive to ridicule, that they often suffer severe mortification. I was often highly amused at the fierce invectives I heard uttered against Mr. Trollope, Basil Hall, and Captain Hamilton. Were any of those individuals to make their appearance in some parts of the Union, their fate certainly would be to be handed over to the jurisdiction of Judge Lynch.

The Americans have many things of which they have just reason to be proud, but when they claim superiority in matters in which they are notoriously deficient, they only expose themselves to well merited ridicule. It is quite amusing to hear how they talk of their literature, their refinement, and their great proficiency in the fine arts. The fact is, America is yet at that stage where the *utilities* of life are the main things attended to. The elegancies, the refined luxuries of life, particularly the literary luxuries which elevate the taste, and cast a charm round society, are yet wanting, and it can scarcely be expected that they should yet be possessed of them. They are all busily engaged in the pursuit of Mammon, striving to outwit, and yet get ahead of, each other in the race after wealth.

There is not, as in England, a numerous class who neither toil nor spin, who are blessed with independent fortunes, whose time is at their own disposal, and whose sole occupation is the rendering their life as agreeable as possible. These are the persons who travel, who study, who indulge in literary leisure, and, who (though the lives of the majority may be spent in frivolous pursuits), erect a standard in sentiment and manners. In this respect the want of the influence of an aristocracy is evidently seen in America. I think it likely that an aristocracy will yet be established either by the steady and gradual progress of the influence of wealth, or by the reaction caused by an overweening democracy.

In all society there is a natural tendency to aristocracy, superior talent, superior industry and knowledge seek to be distinguished by some tangible marks of pre-eminence, while at the same time in a state constituted like America there is an antagonist principle working the other way. There is a desire among the mass to produce a perfect equality by reducing those above them to their own standard. These two principles, though antagonists, may work to the same end.

At present in the United States, democracy is absolutely running to seed and if the popular feeling which at present exists continue for some years longer it will make sad work of the constitution. Anarchy and confusion will ensue, a reaction will then take place. The necessity of public order will at last be perceived. To secure that, a vigorous government will be necessary, and of it an aristocracy of some kind or other will be the natural result. This is mere speculation, but still it is far from improbable and, though the Americans consider their republic as to endure for ages yet, history teaches us to look on no public institution as secure which the mere caprice of a people can affect.

I am convinced that at the present day a popular chief like General Jackson could turn Congress out of doors and establish a military despotism.

The United States Bank question has excited a powerful sensation, and given rise to great difference of opinion which has been expressed in anything but moderate terms. The bulk of the people strenuously support the President in the unyielding stand he has made against that institution, while the majority of the respectable merchants are strongly opposed to his measures and stigmatise them as most injurious to the interests of the country.

General Jackson is opposed to the Bank on the ground of its being a great monied monopoly which might be used as a political engine, and by its powerful interference in elections be wielded with fatal results to the liberties of the people. He wishes to establish a metallic currency and yet in spite of all his effort there is scarcely such a thing as gold to be found in circulation in the United States.

According to the Federal Constitution each state may charter as many banks and issue as much paper as it pleases, but the United States Bank, by its great command of money, had the power of exercising an indirect check upon the states' banks and preventing an excessive issue of notes. That check is now withdrawn, and the consequence in all probability will be that the country will be deluged with paper trash, too great a facility of obtaining money will be afforded to traders, its value will be depreciated, a fictitious prosperity will prevail, and whenever credit receives the slightest shock a general crash must ensue. But, "Hurrah for General Jackson," is the cry now among the mass. This man is so amazingly popular that he could persuade the people almost to anything and he is so ambitious that if he were a younger man, I am convinced he would lead the Americans a *new* dance to the tune of Yankee Doodle.

His enemies say that the warlike attitude which he displayed lately in his negotiations with France arose from his desire to be elected a third time, which certainly would have been the case, so great is the confidence in his military talents. A war with France would have been very popular with the bulk of the people as far as I could learn from conversations I had with every class of people, Members of Congress etc., and that heterogeneous class one meets at the coffee houses, and in the steamboats, and also from the numerous popular caricatures, which are sometimes no bad indices of a nation's feelings. One of these caricatures was an amusing representation of old Hickory dancing over Louis Philippe in a reel called the "Virginia scamper down." The grim old President was footing it away very merrily, and shouting to Van Buren who played first fiddle, "Damn it, Martin, strike up a war dance."

But the wealthy class would have been strongly opposed to war, and with just reason for the American Marine is now so deficient that her trade would have been terribly cut up by the enemy's cruisers.

The policy of the United States is plainly peace. Let her pocket all insults she may receive and devote her energies to the extension of the commerce and the equipment of a powerful fleet to protect it, and thus secure the continuance of peace by the display of her strength.

It is curious to remark the difference that obtains between Irish and English settlers in this country. The Irish are received as brothers, they intermarry and amalgamate with the people and with that happy adaptation to circumstances which distinguishes the Irish character, they soon identify their interests with the country and look upon it as their own. And yet, with this pliability of disposition is joined an unalterable attachment to their native land. America is the country of their adoption, but Ireland is the land of their best love, it is the soil of their birth, in which the bones of their fathers repose, and to it their hearts turn with that fond remembrance which clings round early scenes and early hopes.

Every Irishman whom I met, while he regarded America as his country, and prided himself on being the free citizen of a free state, yet still seemed animated by a strong love for his native land. Many of the leading merchants of New York, Philadelphia, Baltimore, and New Orleans are Irish, and their influence is so great that they are able to turn the scale at almost every election greatly to the discomfiture of the native born who make sad complaints, but there is no redress. Paddy is increasing every day, and this is a free country where every man has his vote.

An Irish labourer one day at an election in New York said with much contempt to a little Yankee who was making a grievous outcry about the hardship of being outridden by a parcel of foreigners: " Bad luck to you, would you hould yer tongue, what is it yer talking about. Sure you were born here and can't help being a citizen, but I came here of my own free will and pleasure and have a better right to the country than you." The Yankee had nothing to say to this triumphant reply, particularly as it was enforced by a very formidable looking shillelagh.

The national talent of " handling the twig " has not degenerated by change of clime. The lower Irish, here, as at home, are distinguished by their great adroitness and agility which they display in the use of the shillelagh, and as there is no police, and it is long before a sufficient body of militia can be mustered to quell a disturbance, the " boys " have generally ample time to break their opponents' heads to the tune of Erin go Bragh.

The Americans are a newspaper reading people and with this species of reading they are abundantly supplied. Even the smallest little village has its print or two whereby the good people are enlightened as to passing events and the cause of this or that party advocated, if not with propriety of language, at least with great vigour of style. The people are all naturally politicians. Their institutions make them so. They are the sole dispensers of rewards and plans; from the frequency of elections they are continually called on to exercise their judgment on public men and public measures; they are made to feel their own importance and the direct interest they have in the common weal.

From the instruction they receive from the papers, the public meetings and daily discussions, they are remarkably well informed on all points that affect their interests, and can speak on them with an acuteness and volubility that astonished me.

They have libel law in America but I believe it is not often resorted to, though there are few countries where the Press revels in such uncontrolled liberty, and where newspapers teem with such gross abuse and ruffian scurrility.

The usual plan to obtain redress for libel (adopted particularly in the Southern and Western States) is both summary and effective. It saves a deal of litigation; the proverbial delays and expenses of the law are avoided, and the matter is brought to a speedy if not satisfactory issue.

The party who considers himself aggrieved provides himself either with a cowhide, a Boey knife, or perhaps shoulders his rifle (according to the measure of the offence, or the irritability of his disposition) and at once proceeds against the delinquent, who, if he should be taken unawares, expiates his offence by having his throat cut, or his body drilled by a rifle bullet. He

may consider himself particularly fortunate if he escape with
a *sound whaling*.

Editors in the United States however, are generally prepared
for such emergencies, and at times very interesting passages
of arms occur between them and the gentlemen with whose
characters they make free.

The Americans are a very unimaginative people. They view
everything with reference to how many dollars and cents they
can make out of it. Take a Yankee to the Falls of Niagara and
instead of being overwhelmed with the sublimity of the scene
he would talk to you of the immense amount of water power,
and of the great natural facilities for manufactories. Place him
on the bank of a rushing river in the midst of one of the boundless forests of his own land, and instead of being affected by
the loneliness and solemn grandeur of the dark woods around
him, he would descant on the richness of the soil, and the
advantages it would afford for a profitable settlement. Take
him to Westminster Abbey, or to any of the venerable
cathedrals of the Continent of Europe, and instead of feeling
his heart awed with reverence and filled with recollections
of the past, he would doubtless be speculating on the value and
cost of the structure.

These remarks apply generally, though of course there are
very many exceptions.

They are continually on the move, the public conveyances
are always crowded and the hotels always full. You, here, see
nothing of the quiet decorum of an English inn. The taverns
here are always filled with a number of restless, noisy, hurrying
people, as if their salvation depended on the haste they made.
Courtesy and politeness are unknown terms. The rule seems
to be that everyone should take care of himself. About half an
hour before dinner the guests assemble at the door of the
dining room, and as soon as the bell rings they rush in like a
pack of hungry wolves, feed with as much voracity as if

they had been famished for weeks, and after having hastily despatched their meal bolt out to the bar room where they amuse themselves picking their teeth with their long knives, chewing tobacco, smoking cigars, and drinking brandy and water.

In the Southern and Western States the laws are not paramount. The people are above the laws and this must be the case for the executive being elected by the people dare not put the laws in force against their own constituents. Everyone goes armed with dagger, Boey knife, or pistols, and sometimes with all three, and in a society where the passions are so little under control it is not to be wondered at that murderous affrays should so often take place in the streets. When I was in Frankfort in Kentucky an election for Member of Congress was held, and during the voting pistols were fired, and knives drawn in the court house in the presence of the governor and hundreds of people, and yet the law never interfered. A person whom I knew intimately was in the habit of taking his meals at the hotel where I stopped. One evening, at supper, he had a dispute with some person about politics, who after a few words had passed, rose, drew his dagger, and stabbed my acquaintance several times. The wounded man fell, and bled profusely, and was carried to bed. He ultimately recovered, but the authorities never interposed, and the assassin was never even questioned. About the same time, at Louisville in the same state, during an election, one of the candidates meeting the other in the street deliberately drew a pistol from his breast and shot him down. The man fortunately was not killed, but severely wounded, yet the assailant was never brought to account. Do not suppose that these ruffianly encounters are confined to the ignorant and comparatively uneducated part of the community — why the highest men of the land are constantly giving example of the same atrocious proceedings. The present President, General Jackson, and one Colonel Benton were at feud, they happened to meet in a tavern. Jackson, without saying a word, drew a pistol, advanced on his opponent and shot him down, and with a second pistol was about giving him the " coup de grace " when he was shot by Benton's brother, who then came forward with a Boey knife to cut Jackson's throat, and would have done so had he not been restrained by the spectators. The other day a mob in Cincinnati pulled down several houses and were never prosecuted. A Negro was lately burned to death over a *slow fire* in Missouri. Several people have been hanged by *Lynch* law in the last month, on *suspicion* merely of being abolitionists, and the law did not, and could not interfere, and yet they talk of their liberty. I am sick of such twaddle. Why, when there are no laws or, what amounts to the same thing, when the laws are not vigorously and impartially administered, there can be no rational liberty.

The character of the American nation is fundamentally that of the British, though greatly modified by circumstances. While they have many of the virtues of the English, they have also their vices *pushed to excess*, and besides several more of their own growth. They possess great intelligence, energy, enterprise, and perseverence, all the elements necessary to make a flourishing commercial people, but they lack the qualities of a noble and generous nation. Their courage degenerates into ferocity, their love of liberty into licentiousness, and their commercial enterprise into a sordid and mercenary spirit. Their duels are always of a very ferocious and sanguinary character. They go out to the field armed with two or three brace of pistols, and fight with the utmost malignity. Most of their encounters terminate fatally. In England when a man " goes out " it is not so much from motives of revenge, as to vindicate his honour and set himself right with society.

When I was in Washington an affair occurred, which I cite as an illustration because from all I have heard the vindictive spirit that was manifested, shocking as it was, is by no means a rare feature in their duels. Two lads, one of them, a midshipman, the other a student of West Point Military Academy, mere boys they were, and had been most intimate friends, unfortunately quarrelled about some trifle. They met, and at the second or third fire, one fell mortally wounded. His opponent went up to him, expressed his sorrow, and entreated him to forgive him before he died. The wounded man with difficulty raised himself on his elbow, and glaring on his antagonist with a look of baffled rage told him that neither there nor in eternity would he ever forgive him, expressed his enmity in terms of the deepest malignity, and sinking back almost immediately afterwards expired with a curse on his lips and a scowl of hatred on his brow.

October 1836

From Buffalo went by railroad to a little village called Tonawanda — 30 miles — from thence to Niagara.

4th October. First looked on the Falls. My anticipations have been more than realised. No language can convey any idea of the grandeur of the scene. The spectator is overwhelmed with admiration and feels himself unable to describe his own emotions. The more I gazed at this wondrous cascade the more was I impressed by its sublimity. I viewed it from every point and still with increased admiration. It is an object to which the eye nor heart could ever become so habituated as to view it with indifference. Though its aspect be little varied and its roar be monotonous, yet one never tires looking at it and listening to its mighty voice.

In ordinary scenes the sound of falling water is inexpressibly soothing to the senses. The rippling of the sea on a pebbly beach, the murmuring of a brook, the gushing of a fountain excite a pleasing feeling, and lull the mind. But Niagara, with its thundering voice and rushing flood mantled in spray and white with foam, absolutely stuns the mind of the spectator, and excites mingled emotions of admiration and awe.

In the language of the Indians Niagara means " thunder of the waters." Some one has compared it to an ocean tumbling over a precipice, but no language can describe its magnificence. Words fail me when I speak of it. It combines in the highest degree, sublimity and beauty — awfully sublime, terribly beautiful. How brightly do its snowy waters flash in the sunshine and the spray cloud that hangs over it sparkle like a glory. " God hath set his rainbow on its forehead " and its deep voice seems to proclaim his Almighty power.

147

Though I will not attempt to describe the Falls, I may at least give you some idea of the localities and leave the rest to your own imagination. The River Niagara is the channel by which the waters of Lakes Superior, Michigan, Huron and Erie empty themselves into Lake Ontario. When you consider the size of these lakes, or rather inland seas, the first being nearly five hundred, and the latter three hundred miles long and nine hundred feet deep, you may form some idea of the immense body of water that is continually passing over the falls. The river is studded with several pretty islands. One of these divides the stream into two branches, forming two separate cataracts nearly at right angles to each other. The one on the Canadian side is from its shape called the Horse-Shoe Fall.

Two or three miles above the Falls the rapids commence. There is then a considerable declivity in the bed of the river and the stream being contracted rushes along with great rapidity, roaring and foaming and tossing high its snowy waves like the sea in a storm, till it arrives near the edge of the precipice where it flows smoothly along as if collecting itself for the wild leap it is about to make into the dread chasm below. The solid earth trembles with the shock, and a cloud of spray rises high into the air, and is visible at the distance of thirty or forty miles.

Between the two cataracts is a rock on the verge of the precipice, and at the extremity of the American fall, a high tower has been erected. The view from the top of this is very grand, a kind of bridge or platform runs from the base of the tower and projects several feet over the falls. I gained the extremity of it and looked down on the whirling pool below. This narrow platform was wet and slippery, very crazy and leaning much to one side, so that it was rather a hazardous thing to walk along it. If a person were to make a single false step on it, in an instant he would be swept like a withered leaf over the falls. It is called the Terrapin Bridal, I suppose from its resemblance to the back of a tortoise. Having viewed the falls from every point of view on the American side, I crossed to the Canadian shore. One of the grandest views is from the centre of the shore there, where the little skiff is dancing like a bubble on the agitated and foam covered water, a cataract tumbling down on the right hand and another on the left; nothing to be seen but sky and rocks and water; you are surrounded by the wild magnificence and feel yourself mingled with the sublimity of the scene.

But the sight of sights : the crowning wonder of the whole, is to pass behind the grand sheet of falling water. This is an exploit which I had heard represented as dangerous, both from the narrowness of the ledge on which you walk and from the occasional falling of detached pieces of rock from above. However, I determined on trying it and found both the danger and difficulty greatly exaggerated. I went to the guide's house on the top of the rock to make preparations, and while I was undressing preparatory to putting on an oilskin dress, two Scotch gentlemen came in. Having just been under the fall they looked like drowned rats, so wet and " drookit " and miserable did they appear. They represented it as an " awfu " undertaking on such a day and wished me a pleasant bath and safe back again. Being fully rigged out in a suit of oil cloth, an oiled hat tied down over my ears, strong shoes to protect my feet, and a belt round my waist, I descended the rock with my guide. Having arrived near the fall, the guide (a Negro) addressed me : " Now massa, shut am mouth, hold down am head, and look to am's feet, rock in dis place berry slippery I tink." I followed his directions, and in we plunged through the blinding spray. I had not proceeded many paces when I heard him with a wheezing cough, and exclaiming in a half choked voice, " Oh, ah, Garamighty very dam cold," and it was indeed the coldest operation I ever endured. We were in

an instant drenched to the skin, the water that fell on our
heads seemed to penetrate to the very brain and the wind
was sharp and cutting. Having arrived at termination rock
when all further progress is barred, I was able to look around
me and behold by the dim light that struggled through the
water the surpassing magnificence of the scene. I stood on a
narrow ledge of rock. Behind me was the precipice from which
the torrent leaped out over my head, not having the appearance
of falling in a regular sheet but tumbling down in immense
avalanche-like masses of white water, so close to me that I
could almost have put out my hand and touched it, while
beneath me was the fearful pool whirling and boiling and
sending up clouds of smoke like spray. Sambo, who was standing shivering at my side, his teeth going like a pair of
castanets, and his face of a pepper and salt complexion, wisely
observed it was bad for one's health to stand long there, and
proposed that we should retrace our steps. After having
dressed, and got from Mr. Starkie a glass of brandy and water,
and a formal certificate to the effect that I had performed the
exploit of passing under the sheet of water, I visited the
museum, which contains a collection of natural curiosities
found in the neighbourhood of the Falls. The proprietor
obligingly sells any article his visitors may fancy, at not more
than ten times its value. Stopped three days at Niagara and
left it with regret. Went to Lewiston, from thence across Lake
Ontario to Toronto, a distance of forty or fifty miles.

Toronto seated on the shore of the lake—neat little city,
population 9,000. Waited on the Governor, was struck with
the contrast between Yankee hotels and the one I stopped at
here. Several retired British officers at the house. Pleasant
and social circle of well-informed, gentlemanlike men, very
different from those I have some times been in the habit of
meeting.

Hired a horse, the best I could get, but still a very sorry

steed, to make an excursion through the western part of the province. I had not ridden far when I discovered that my Rosinante was a very stumbling piece of horse flesh. He made several most determined attempts to break my neck, and his own knees. Stopped the first night at a little hamlet situated in a deep ravine, called Sixteen Mile Creek. Next morning started early and got to Mr. Sheddans before they were up, found Henry there, stopped a day and then proceeded towards Port Dover. Benighted in a pine forest, sorely perplexed for some time. At last dismounted, threw the reins on the horse's neck (he was too much fatigued to run away from me) followed him and at last came to a clearing. A light gleamed in the distance at sight of which the horse neighed apparently with great satisfaction and trotted towards it. I pursued and found a cottage where I passed the night. Next day passed through Brandtford, a prettily situated little village — only a few years founded — this was the residence of Brandt, the Mohawk chief. The Mohawk village lies at the distance of three miles from this on the grand river.

These Indians have made considerable advance in civilization. They are Christians, have a church, and schoolhouse, engage in agricultural pursuits, and live in the greatest harmony and good feeling with their white neighbours. In fact, all the Canadian Indians are quiet inoffensive people. They are kindly and justly treated and look on the whites with perfect confidence, whereas, in the States, the policy of the government and the conduct of the people have been such as to excite in the Indians a most deep rooted abhorrence of the Yankees.

The Mohawks are possessed of a fine tract of country. Stayed at Brandtford all night. Next evening reached Port Dover, six or seven miles distant from Mr. Moore's. After riding some time in the dark through the wood, found it impossible to get on as the horse was continually running foul of the stumps and fallen trees, contrived to get on the beach which was very narrow and shingly. The lake was very boisterous and the waves dashed so far up as scarcely to leave me a foot of dry shore to ride on. It came on to rain and blow with great violence.

> " That night a child might understand
> The De'il had business on his hand."

It was so pitchy dark, I could not see the horse's head. He stumbled at every step and sometimes fell. Immense trees that had been blown down lay across the beach, and extended far into the water. To get past them I was obliged to put the horse into the lake, and sometimes swim round them. He was so frightened by the dashing of the waves that it required whip and spur to urge him to this. After toiling slowly along for about two hours, came slap against a great tree that barred my path. The horse obstinately refused to go far enough into the water, and beginning to plunge, lost his footing and came down. I then attempted to ride him up the wooded bank and having surmounted the ascent he dashed at something and fell head foremost among the branches of a fallen tree. I got my feet out of the stirrups but in attempting to rise, I jammed my leg so tightly among the branches that I could not extricate myself, the horse meantime, kicking and struggling to dis-entangle *himself* had worked himself round, till his head lay at my shoulder. I feared if he succeeded in getting up and leaping forward as he was attempting to do he would come right slap on me and smash me. While I was remonstrating with him and endeavouring to " soothe " him, he partly dis-entangled himself and plunging forward struck me with his head or shoulder so violently as to drive me bang against the trunk of a tree with such force as to knock the fire from my eyes and make me feel as if I was " kilt outright." After recovering and considering whether it was best to remain there quietly till morning, or make another attempt, I determined on returning to the beach, and after about another hour's plunging and struggling succeeded in reaching Mr. Moore's. The sight of a blazing fire was very refreshing. I must have appeared in very miserable plight, I was cold and dripping with wet, my hat was crushed close on my head and my clothes soiled. Mr. and Mrs. Moore were in bed, but the young ladies were seated round the fire. I introduced myself to them and told them my mishaps. Mr. M. soon appeared. I was received with a genuine Irish welcome—in a few minutes I was rigged out in a dry dress and was relating my adventures over a tumbler of punch.

Mr. Moore's farm consists of two hundred acres. Most of it is forest, but he expects by next year to have seventy or eighty acres cleared. In the course of a few years they will be very comfortable here, but at present they must endure great inconvenience, and the ladies particularly must surely feel the want of many comforts to which they had been accustomed. However, they appear to have adapted themselves wonderfully to altered circumstances and, if not absolutely content, they at least bear the change with light and cheerful spirits. It is nothing for man to rough it but it is melancholy to see a woman who has been gently nurtured exposed to the hardships of a life in the woods, deprived of all society, and even obliged to perform the menial offices of the house. Stopped a day and two nights at Mr. Moore's and returned by way of Hamilton, which is very prettily situated on Burlington Bay and surrounded by high wooded hills. The country a short distance on each side of the road I travelled, is well settled. The farm houses are neat and comfortable with every appearance of plenty about them. Soil principally a sandy loam, produces good crops considering the very indifferent way in which it is cultivated — twenty to thirty bushels of wheat per acre — forty and fifty bushels of oats—250 to 300 bushels of potatoes. One great drawback is that they cannot grow Indian corn with any certainty, it is a most valuable grain. The straw is nutritious fodder for cattle while the corn is easily dressed and in various shapes forms wholesome food for man. The last day of my ride the horse was so bedraggled that I could scarcely get him along. At last had to dismount and drag him after me.

After stopping a few days at Toronto, Henry joined me and we started for Lake Simcoe, forty miles distant, crossed the lake and established our headquarters at Barrie. This is an embryo town containing as yet only a few wooden houses, the oldest of which has not been more than three years built. Very comfortably fixed in an Englishman's house. We enjoy our rambles very much and have become such experienced woods-men that we can take a day's march thro' the trackless forest. From early morning till night we are in the bush. The woods are now arrayed in their gorgeous Autumn livery. The leaves are of every tint from the pale yellow of the walnut to the bright crimson of the red oak and wild vine, while the dark green of the pine and cedar contrast well with the bright tints of the deciduous trees. About a fortnight ago the colouring of the forest was still more rich and beautiful. Now the leaf has become too sear, and the dead foliage scattered by every blast and thickly strewing the ground exercises a melancholy influ-ence on the mind, and impresses it with a sense of desolation and decay. There is a peculiar stillness and loneliness in the woods now which is saddening and yet pleasing to the heart. Sometimes, even on the calmest day you hear the wind pass through the naked tree tops with a sighing tone which is inexpressibly melancholy. It sounds as if the spirit of the forest were mounting over its decay.

I am delighted with these vast woods, they are so wild and free. I can easily conceive the unquenchable love which the Indian bears to them. It is the same powerful attachment that binds the Swiss to his mountains, bleak and barren though they be, a sentiment which is never felt with equal force by the inhabitants of level or well-cultivated countries.

Walking through the bush is very fatiguing from the great quantity of fallen timber over which one is obliged to climb. I have sometimes become entangled in windfalls; to disengage oneself from an extensive one is almost a day's work.

These are occasioned by a blast of wind striking some part of the forest with such force that everything is prostrated before it. The mighty trees are torn up by the roots, crashed and rended and piled on each other in wild confusion.

One day, came upon a tract of forest two or three miles square. The mouldering logs and the blackened fire scathed stumps presented a very melancholy appearance. What a very grand sight the conflagration must have been! Imagine the roaring and crackling of the flames, and the terror and astonishment of the wild beasts. One day separated from Henry by a windfall. After toiling for hours through thickets and over fallen trees, steering my course by the sun, came to a piece of table land which was quite clear of trees. From the elevation I had a magnificent view. Beneath me lay the dark woods, stretching away in an unbroken mass as far as the eye could reach and bounded in the distance by the blue mountains of the Huron. The spot where I stood had been an Indian battle ground — the trees that skirted it were thickly marked by bullets. Many a head had, there, been despoiled of its scalp. Fired my rifle as a signal to Harry who happens to be in hearing, and soon afterwards joined me. Descended the eminence to the low ground, passed on through a cedar swamp, where our further progress was barred by a dark deep stream that flowed sluggishly along thro' the overarching woods. We found two canoes drawn up among the weeds. They were made of birchen bark and were of slender and elegant make, and so light as to be easily carried. They belonged to some roaming Indians, who were, I suppose, on a hunting excursion. Cedar swamps, silent

gloomy solitude, almost unpenetrable from the close inter-
laced branches and the fallen and decaying timber. Sometimes,
in the heart of these wildernesses, I have chanced upon a lonely
little spot, carpeted with luxuriant moss, far softer than the
richest Turkey rug, and glowing in the sunshine which poured
down through the parted branches overhead.

Visited one day a little lake of about three miles in circumference. It was surrounded by such thick cedar woods that it
was no easy matter to reach it. Got wet in the swamps and
made a fire to warm ourselves. It was freezing keen and Henry,
not liking to sit in wet trousers took them off and hung them
up before the fire to dry. He presented a very picturesque
appearance wanting his unutterables. We have become very
hardy and don't mind the cold.

Barrie is beautifully situated on the extremity of an arm of
the lake. Sometimes, on returning from our daily excursions,
I have reached a range of elevated ground behind the village
just as the sun was sinking behind the tree tops like a globe of
fire, and been greatly charmed with the lovely scene that lay
beneath me. The clear smooth waters of the bay lying in the
entrance of the dark and silent woods, the thin smoke from the
hamlet rising high into the air, and perhaps a group of cows
on the margin of the water, presented an appearance of beautiful repose.

We feel very comfortable in our quarters, our host and his
wife are very attentive. They have been in better circumstances have only lately settled here and have all those English
notions of comfort, neatness and cleanliness which are very
rarely met with in the bush.

Every night on coming home, we find a cheerful fire blazing
on the capacious hearth, and have a plentiful dinner served up
to which our walk enables us to do very ample justice. But I
must describe our quarters more minutely. Our room is rather
large for a log house, it runs the whole breadth of the building.

It has a window at each end, one of which looks towards the lake, and the other to the yard in which, if it were daylight, you might see a pet fawn, a flock of turkeys, and three or four very corpulent pigs which our host has serious intentions of converting into bacon and hams before long.

Suppose yourself looking in upon us after dinner—you see the table furnished with glasses, a jug of hot water and a decanter of Canadian whiskey, a shocking bad-tasted, though mild and wholesome spirit. We have mixed a glass of punch and are trying to persuade ourselves that it is Innishowen. Round the boarded walls hang several deers' antlers, trophies of the chase, in one corner is a shelf with a few books, some pieces of cracked delft, a powder horn and bunch of knitting needles. Our guns rest against the walls, and lying beside them are bullet pouches, belts and two formidable looking hunting knives. On one side of the fire sits Henry, on the other, myself. Henry is luxuriantly taking his ease with his heels resting against the wall, and elevated considerably above his head. This is a mode of indulgence he learned in Yankee land. On returning late one evening from a long walk in the woods, we found a gentleman in our room who congratulated himself on our arrival. Said he had travelled far, was excessively hungry and asked permission to join us at dinner, which he assured us was quite ready. He had been impatiently watching the progress of its being cooked. He introduced himself to us as Captain M. of His Majesty's Navy, and according to his own account, a most distinguished officer; he afforded us great amusement; such a compound of self sufficient vanity, pompous egotism and loquacious mendacity, I never before had the luck to meet. He was a very curious leaf of that book "human nature." He ate prodigiously, drank profoundly, and talked incessantly. In the course of the evening, he told as many bouncing lies as would have filled a quarto volume.

He had travelled in every clime, and been the hero of numberless strange adventures, in every country under the known world. Baron Munchausen was quite an ordinary personage, compared with him. He had hunted tigers in India, lions in South Africa, and bears in Russia, in company with his particular friend Prince Maschurewich. Among other illustrious individuals with whom he was acquainted was the Grand Cham of Tartary. He had been at a very pleasant dinner party on the top of the Great Pyramid, travelling across the desert once, the caravan was attacked by Arabs and he made his escape on the back of an ostrich etc. Such were the sort of stories he entertained us with to our irrepressible mirth, and he concluded amidst copious draughts of brandy and water to descant on the virtues of temperance.

November 1836

Frozen up at Barrie; on account of the ice, boat could not cross the lake; walked through the woods thirty miles to Holland landing and from that by wagon to Toronto, bright, cold, bracing weather.

Present at the opening of the House of Assembly by the Governor.

14th November. Left Toronto by steamboat St. George. Next morning arrived at Kingston where the steamer stopped two hours, we had intended to remain some days at Kingston but winter is setting in so rapidly that fearing the navigation might be stopped, we determined to hasten on to Montreal. Called on Dr. Sampson — he received us in a frank and cordial manner and expressed his regret (in a way which showed they were not mere words of course) that we could not stop some days with him.

Kingston, small place, prettily situated — Arsenal — fort — barracks.

Soon after leaving Kingston entered the St. Lawrence, passed thro' what is called the " Lake of the Thorn Isles." The river here is thickly studded with beautiful little wooded isles. In Summer the scenery must be exquisite — the noble river gemmed over with these flower enammeled leafy islets must present a picture of matchless loveliness and almost make the traveller think he is in the midst of enchantment and sailing past fairy bowers.

17th November. Arrived at Montreal on the 17th, called on Mr. Knox; he has been very attentive to us, got horses, and in company with him took a ride of twenty-five miles through the island. Behind the city is a mountain from which it takes

159

its name. The view from this hill is very fine, embracing the city with its glittering spires. The stately St. Lawrence, and its foaming rapids, and wooded isles, and far away, blue and indistinct, the mountains of Vermont. Streets of Montreal, narrow — houses well built of handsome grey stone — number of churches — large cathedral — four or five convents. Country about the city well cleared and tolerably well cultivated. The lands are held principally in perpetuity under the Seigniori, the tenants rendering a small rent and certain feudal services. The Lower Canadians are an amiable, inoffensive people but ignorant and indolent in the extreme, and so wedded to old habits and prejudices that it is almost impossible to induce them to adopt any improvement. The superior industry and intelligence of the British settler will ultimately dispossess them all.

Papineau possesses great influence. He is amazingly popular with the people. The object of his agitation is to render the legislative Council Elective, which would throw the Government of the country entirely into the hands of his party.

The Canadians are not prepared for the political privileges which they do possess. I have been told that a majority of the House of Assembly cannot even write their names.

The costume of the people is very comfortable and looks well. They wear a grey or red cap, grey great coat belted with a red sash and high boots.

Houses well provided against the cold, double windows, stoves in lobbies, flues through the different apartments.

Winter in Canada is the season of amusement. Business is then at a stand. The ground is covered with frozen snow to such a depth that all irregularities are filled up, and the country presents an even white surface over which they can travel in their sleighs with great velocity. The sleighs are fitted up with buffalo robes and bear skins and the harness of the horses are hung with bells to give notice of their approach. They are very fond of this mode of travelling. They say the rapidity of the motion and the merry sound of the bells make it very exhilarating. I have heard however that you may form a very good idea of the pleasures of sleighing if you just sit down in a thorough draught of air, put your feet in a tub of cold water and jingle the poker and tongs together.

The moose, which is plenty in some parts of Lower Canada is one of the largest of the deer species, it is very wary and difficult of access. It is generally in winter that it is taken. Equipped in snow shoes which enable him to move more easily over the surface of the snow, the hunter follows the trail of the animal sometimes for days before he comes up with it. The moose is impeded in its motions by its feet breaking through the upper crust of snow and is at last exhausted and run down.

Left Montreal 23rd of November in company with Mr. Park whom we happened to meet at our hotel. When we left the wharf the morning was grey and cloudy, but we had scarcely reached the middle of the river when the sun broke brightly forth and gave a cheerful aspect to everything. The city appeared to great advantage, its situation is very good. It extends a considerable distance along the river with the mountain in the back ground and the wooded island of St. Helens in front.

The steamers on the St. Lawrence are very good boats, clean and well appointed. By steamer to La Prairie nine miles thence by railroad eighteen miles to St. Johns, where we got on board the Franklin, which was fitted up in a style of scrupulous neatness, everything was in apple pie order. The captain's office was like a little temple, profusely decorated with china and glass ornaments, rare seaweed and shells, artificial flowers etc. The captain was quite in keeping with the furniture. The choice of his dress had evidently cost him serious deliberation and the arrangement of it no little trouble. His whiskers were oiled and curled, and the delicate blush on his cheek plainly announced that the rouge pot was one of the articles of his toilet. He moved about with the mincing step of a *Petit Maitre*, evidently on the very best terms with himself and looking as spruce and unruffled as if he had just stepped out of a band box. The stewardess was pranked out in an antique looking rustling silk gown. She wore a high standing Queen Elizabeth ruff and her hair was piled up to an awful height, something like the " system " which I have heard old ladies describe. And the steward, an amazingly fine mannered personage glided about like a master of the ceremonies, with noiseless step, and insinuating manner, receiving all commands with a smile and executing them with officious politeness.

At supper six or seven good looking boys dressed as pages, and wearing fancy caps ornamented with silver bands and tassels, attended, skipping about and supplying the wants of the guests with the greatest activity, and even anticipating their wishes.

After we had supped, the black gentlemen came below and had their meal. In this land of liberty, the blacks, no matter what may be their station, are not allowed to mix with the white Massas.

Lake Champlain 140 miles long, greatest breadth not more than twelve miles. Its scenery, if not grand, is highly picturesque. It is skirted by a range of hills of such dimensions that they might be dignified with the name of mountains, several beautiful glens lie amongst them about twenty miles from the lower end of the lake. It narrows so much that there is scarcely more than room for the boat to turn. Its course is very serpentine, winding along like a silvery snake among the wooded hills, and presenting at every turn a new and beautiful landscape. Not at all expecting such scenery, I was agreeably surprised.

In the early part of the day there was a snowstorm, the drifting snow and the heavy masses of vapour which rolled along the tops of the mountains by concealing their real altitude, left something to the imagination, and gave additional effect to the scenery.

Reached Whitehall next morning, took canal boat to Troy. Distance seventy miles—a curious mode of conveyance, easy enough, you glide along as smoothly as a placid stream, but as monotonously. Strange mixture of passengers, we were all rammed, crammed and jammed together in a low narrow cabin which had a table down the centre and lockers on each side. The following injunction in large letters was posted up in two or three places: " Gentlemen, you must keep your feet off the seats." There were about thirty gentlemen and twenty ladies, by courtesy so called. The apartment of the latter was separated from ours by a green baize curtain, which concealed them from our sight but did not prevent us hearing the clack of their tongues.

When bedtime came, boards were fastened horizontally along the sides with hooks and ropes, forming with the lockers three tiers and looking exactly like shelves in a woollen draper's shop—it was a very funny contrivance.

When all was ready the captain (!!) called our names from the list, and each person in the order in which he then stood, had his choice of a berth. I was near the head of the list and having an early choice, I selected one of the lowest tier, preferring to run the chance of my two upper neighbours breaking down on me to being suffocated by the heated air and unsavoury smells which would naturally ascend. There was so little space between these comical berths that it was no easy matter to get into them. Once you had effected a location, you might be said literally to be laid on the shelf. You were obliged to make yourself as small as possible and to lie still for if you lifted your head three inches from the pallet it struck against the berth above.

One corpulent old fellow made choice of one of the lowest.

Indeed any of the others to him would have been quite in-
accessible. After he had bundled himself in with great difficulty,
and with many a groan, he began to reflect that perhaps his
situation was not without danger. Lying on his back with his
eyes raised apprehensively he exclaimed in a very uneasy tone
of voice, " but captain I cal'clate I'm in a bad fix here. If these
two gentlemen break down on me, I guess I shall be knocked
into immortal smash." I thought the little doghole of a cabin
would have been insufferably hot, but that night it froze
intensely, and though I lay in my clothes with my pea jacket
over me, I felt it very cold. At five o'clock next morning,
arrived at Troy. This is a good-looking town, pleasantly situated on the Hudson, clean and well built.

Left Troy by the conveyance which was provided for us by
the steamboat agent, and although we had nearly two hours
to go a distance of six miles, owing to the stoppages made by
the driver, we were too late getting to Albany. Just as we drove
to the wharf, we saw the steamer going off. We demanded of
the agent to have our money returned, which he refused, but
said we should have a passage of the boat next day. We wasted
a great deal of eloquent indignation on him, but he was a cool
imperturbable Yankee, smoked his segar and listened, quite un-
concerned, to the unsavoury epithets that were bestowed on
him.

Albany, capital of New York State—old Dutch settlement—
very prettily situated on the Hudson, well built, neat town.
Several good public buildings. In the Town Hall there is a
monument to Sir Walter Scott. The feeling that prompted the
erection of it is very creditable to the Albany people but the
work itself is very unworthy. It is a paltry piece of plaster of
Paris with this inscription: " The citizens of Albany to the
memory of Sir Walter Scott." In the same apartment is a statue
in *wood* of General Hamilton. The Americans who boast so
much of their proficiency in the fine arts should make their

monuments of more lasting materials. From the high ground on which part of the city is built, there is a pretty panoramic view of the surrounding country which is pleasingly diversified by swells and slopes, and there the " Lordly Hudson " rolling its majestic stream along, is itself a sight worth gazing at. Albany, to my mind, is the handsomest city I have seen in America.

26th. Left by the steamer Swallow — a remarkably fine boat — speed fifteen miles an hour. Five-hundred passengers on board, some of them rare specimens.

The Americans are without doubt a very peculiar looking people. Their features are generally good enough, but there is an indescribable something about them, independent of their figures, which strongly characterises them. There is no word I can think of, expresses this peculiarity so well as Yankyishness.

At supper there was a great scramble for places and plates. A stranger viewing them at feeding time would scarcely give them credit for the great polish and politeness to which they pretend. A number of extra berths had to be made. The cabin was literally choke full. We had taken the precaution to secure our berths the day before and were as comfortable as circumstances would admit of, and no little amused with the incidents around us.

27th. Arrived at New York. Whether it is the force of contrast or not, I don't know but the city appears a much finer place than the first time I visited it.

Broadway is very gay. It is the fashionable promenade and is crowded from an early hour till evening with gaily dressed ladies. There is a considerable sprinkling of pretty faces among them but such figures, Oh, ye Graces, after what models were the New York ladies fashioned. Such flat, lanky, awkward figures, only to be equalled by their vile mode of walking. I protest on my conscience, I have not yet seen a woman here who could walk even passably. They have no elasticity of step, not even the shadow of grace in their movements, they have a loose slip shod gait which is the very reverse of the poetry of motion. Some of them do attempt the short step, and lively tripping walk of the French ladies, but all they can accomplish is a painful wriggle. Yet they are celebrated for their style — a Devilish bad style it is. They dress in the most extravagant manner, there is an air of vulgar flash about them which I dislike, they are very partial to fine bonnets. It struck me as not in very good taste for ladies in the depth of winter to wear white silk bonnets bedecked with a profusion of artificial flowers, and ostrich, and Bird of Paradise plumes. I suppose they go on the principle that fine feathers make fine birds. In some circles of New York society you meet ladies of highly cultivated minds and literary attainments, and in the enjoyment of their society you almost forget that they are perhaps a little too cerulean in hue.

Our first call was on Mr. Sampson; found him confined to his room and looking miserably ill, he cannot live long. Death is written on his brow.

28th. At the Mr. N. Our meeting was like that of old friends. Spent the evening there — unfortunately R. was absent.

Called on Miss L., a lady we had met at Baltimore. Were agreeably surprised at finding the Misses A. there. At two or three pleasant parties at Mr. L's.

December 1836

Engaged our passage on board the West Chester. A perfectly new ship that had never been out of dock. She was to have sailed on the 6th. We took leave of our friends, got on board, and thought we were fairly off, but after being towed out about a mile, came to anchor. The captain said most of the crew were drunk and that he could not go to sea. We returned on shore for the day and witnessed the funeral of General Morton. Military procession, great display of militia, they were well armed and clothed, looked very respectable and were a thousand times superior to our Yeomanry.

7th. Came on board, wind ahead, no start today.

8th. Weighed anchor and off at last, bright cold morning, wind fair, all sails set. We are just clearing Sandy Hook and getting out into the open sea, fairly boxed up. Don't like this craft at all, the cabin (a poop one) is small and smells most abominably of paint and varnish. When the door is closed, the heat from the stove is suffocating, and when it is open the frost wind whistles in, setting our teeth a chattering and making our *physiogs* look blue.

There are seventy steerage passengers on board and in our cabin are an ancient maiden lady, two elderly gentlemen, and three others beside ourselves. We have no room to spare. The captain who is of the regular Yankee build, reminds me of a congor eel. In a few days we shall have taken each other's measure. I hope we may agree. We all collected for the first time at dinner. The captain took his seat at the head of the table. Before him was a tureen of very bilious looking pea soup. He began to serve it round, and then as if struck with a sudden thought whispered something to Mr. L. (an Irish priest) who

167

whispered to him and then the captain said: " Gentlemen, if you have no objection, Mr. L. ask a blessing."

" I have no objection," said one and " I have none," said another. " It's all the same to me," said a third. And " I don't care," said a fourth. Whereupon Mr. L. blushed to the very tip of his nose and said grace. The old lady after taking a little soup, laid down her spoon with a look of unutterable anguish. There was evidently something wrong. Her face grew white first and then it grew blue and then it changed to the complexion of the pea soup before her. A crisis was approaching. She screwed her mouth hard, started from the table and made off with great precipitation to her state room. Just as she reached the door, the vessel gave a heel and shot her in head foremost and heels up. A most embarrassing situation for an elderly lady. During dinner we heard her making strange noises and bemoaning her fate in the most piteous terms.

A short time afterwards Mr. L. rose with a very serious air. " Mr. L., where are you going?" but Mr. L. had no time for reply. He popped hurriedly into his cabin and was soon busily engaged clearing up the mysteries of his inner man. It is very amusing to see a person suffering from sea sickness, their distress is so ludicrous that it is impossible to sympathise with them. Mr. L. is a very sapient gentleman, tells self-evident truths, and makes commonplace remarks with an air of the most profound wisdom. He will be quite a jewel on board. I expect great amusement from him.

Mr. W. is a cockney dealer in dry goods. He enlarges very much on his extensive business and in his conversation takes the most unwarrantable liberties with the King's English.

Mr. H. I take to be the editor of a country newspaper. He has all the glibness and self sufficiency of a village politician, and a plentiful lack of ideas. It is a rich treat to hear him and Mr. L. discussing any point, they generally have some deep question under consideration.

Mr. B. is a fattish, lethargic looking old gentleman, with a bald head and large, dull grey eyes. He is very partial to his pipe. When he is not sleeping, he is smoking, and when he sleeps there is no mistake. His apoplectic snore is heard above the dash of the waters and the piping of the wind. But the best of the lot is an old Oxfordshire farmer. He had some intention of emigrating with his family to America, but before taking such an important step, determined to visit the country first and reconnoitre it. He did so, went some distance up the Erie Canal, stopped at some place for a week or two, and then, disgusted with what he had seen, hastened back to New York, got on board this ship and is now in great heart to find himself on the way to England, which he maintains to be the only country in the world worth living in.

13th. In calm weather there are few incidents to break the monotony of a sea voyage. The same regular routine is performed every day, and time glides imperceptibly away. Since we started we have been particularly fortunate in having a favourable wind and plenty of it. We have been lying our course, rattling along at a slapping pace, and have every prospect of making a quick voyage.

15th. It blows fresh and fair, half a gale, the sky is clear and blue without a cloud. The heavy seas crested with foam are tumbling about like so many sea monsters, spitting in our faces as they roll away in huge masses to leeward, and the ship is rushing through the water at the rate of twelve knots an hour, flinging from her bow clouds of spray as she plunges forward in her rapid course.

In looking over the side of the vessel on the dark deep sea, I often find my fancy busy speculating on the secrets that lie far down in the calm blue depths of ocean: the submarine forests, the coral caves, the glittering shells, and gems that strew the sands of the deep.

For the last twenty-four hours we have been carrying on at the rate eleven knots an hour.

16th. Still blows hard. Weather thick and hazy, colder than we have yet felt it. We have now crossed the Banks of Newfoundland. How the vessel heels. I am sitting with my legs against the berth and my back against the door of my state room, trying to preserve my equilibrium while I write. The crockery in the steward's room is jingling and smashing and the old lady in the next state room (out of which she has not moved since she beat her retreat from the dinner table) is alternately *puking* and praying.

The state rooms, as they are called, are by no means the grand apartments the name would lead you to suppose, the one in which I sit is about six feet long and two feet and a half broad, exclusive of the berth. As I sit I am obliged to screw myself up with my knee unpleasantly approximated to my chin.

17th. Sea indescribably uproarious.

18th. The wind has moderated, but still the sea runs high. Just as I was writing the last sentence, heard some one sing out that a vessel in distress was in sight. Went on deck and saw about two or three miles to leeward a vessel apparently under bare poles. At times she was visible as she rose on the crest of a wave; at times concealed from our view in the trough of the sea. We bore down for her and in a short time, ran close under her stern but the sea was too rough to admit of boarding her.

She was a timber laden brig, water logged, and presented a very melancholy spectacle. Her topmasts were carried away, her sails hung in tatters from the yards, her bulwarks were stove in, and as she rattled heavily in the angry sea the waves broke over her sweeping her from stem to stern.

There was no living creature on board. The crew doubtless

had perished. In a short time we had left far behind us the melancholy spectacle on the lonely waters.

This is a delightful night, the moon shines almost as bright as day. The wind has died away. The sea has lost its angry appearance and rolls along in heavy swells. To a landsman it would appear as if the storm had raved itself to rest, and the waves were smoothing themselves after their violent commotion, but the captain says we shall have a strong breeze before morning.

19th. As the skipper foretold, the wind is up again and the sea in a foam. We are lying our course, however, and are bounding merrily along. If this wind lasts, and no accident occurs, we shall soon make the Channel.

20th. Captain had an observation today—ten degrees from Cape Clear. If this breeze stands, in two days we shall see the " fair hills of Holy Ireland."

Christmas Day—The heaviest gale and roughest sea we have yet experienced.

29th. The last four days we have been " lying to." The wind is still ahead and blowing tremendously, had it not been for this unfortunate change, we should have had a very quick passage.

January 1837

5th January. River Mersey — a steamboat came along side — Henry and I took advantage of the opportunity and thus got to Liverpool before the ship, which did not arrive till three days afterwards, having been nearly ashore and lost both anchors. Once more in merry England. The land of rational liberty, and public order, and above all the land of comfort. Everything I see tells me I am not in America. The atmosphere is thick and foggy, the clouds dark and charged with moisture, unlike the clear blue skies of the New World, but then, how green the fields are here. It is quite refreshing to look at them and every man I meet bears good evidence of comfortable living, with his plump person, fresh complexion, and well fed face, presenting a striking contrast to the lank figures and yellow skin-dried visages of the Trans-Atlantickers. It is easy to see that John Bull is a beef eating, porter swilling, hearty buck; while Jonathan is a dram drinking, tobacco chewing " crittur."

As the Derry steamer will not sail on the appointed day, we shall be some time longer in Liverpool than we anticipated. On Sunday, we were waiting on George's Pier for the starting of the ferryboat to Tranmen where we were going to dine, and were very much amused by the manœuvres of the Irishmen who were endeavouring to get a drove of pigs on board. The drivers were genuine boys from the sod, dressed in stout frieze coats, corduroy unutterables, ungartered stockings that hung half way down the leg in a style of graceful negligence exposing part of their brawny limbs. Old Caubeens garnished with a short pipe and stuck on the head with a very *degagé* air completed their costume.

It requires a world of ingenuity to drive pigs. People may suppose it is a simple affair, little do they know of the mysteries of pig driving. A pig-driver is a philosopher, an acute observer of nature, a skilful swayer of the passions and prejudices of the swinish multitude. Many a statesman might take lessons in government from a pig driver. He is an unerring physiognomist. His knowledge of that science would put Lavater to the blush. He not only knows every pig in his herd by the expression of its countenance, but he knows its habits and dispositions, its talents. A pig driver is a great man. I never meet one but I feel disposed to take off my hat and do homage to superior intellect.

The Munster people, along with their many other good qualities, seem all to be born with a talent for the profession. How many grunters under their skilful guidance annually travel along the broad highways and shady lanes of merry England? From the time that the drover leaves his native land, till he has disposed of his stock, what perils does he encounter, what difficulties does he overcome? At first starting what perverseness, obstinacy, and insubordination are manifested by the entire squad? But before he has them a week under his charge, he reduces the most refractory to obedience, and makes them travel together with wonderful unanimity. Sometimes, to be sure, that seditious spirit, which, I suppose, is the result of original sin, will show itself, but the master mind of the drover soon represses it. The gentleman, whose exploits I witnessed, had under his charge upwards of fifty as unsophisticated grunters as ever vexed the heart and tried the patience of man. His object was to get them on board the ferryboat to take them to the Cheshire side. He knew the aversion which pigs have to acquatic excursions, and was well aware of the difficulties he had to encounter. He wore the air of a man who was seriously impressed with the arduous nature of his undertaking, and determined to carry his point. He, himself, armed with a

long whip, was posted on the right wing, his second in command presided over the left. They reached one of the draw
bridges, the herd stopped, it was a moment of deep suspense,
they seemed to be deliberating whether to proceed or fly. The
drover cracked his whip, the hogs obeyed the signal and pushed
on at a smart trot, he hanging on the rear and urging them
forward, apparently with the intention of running them on
board, before they had time for reflection. He evidently anticipated the success of his manœuvre for he called out in a tone
of triumph to his assistant, " I tould you I'd desave the bastes,"
but he reckoned without his host. Soon as the advanced guard
reached the break of the pier, they recoiled aghast at sight of
the peril on which they had been so thoughtlessly rushing. The
drover urged them forward, not a step would they move. The
spirit of opposition was fairly roused. They set their faces
against it, they seemed determined to die rather than go on.
He then changed his tone. He attempted to cajole them, he
coaxed them, he flattered them, he called them all the pet
names in his vocabulary, but in vain. One long-sided, sharp-
snouted old hog, who seemed to be the ringleader of the party,
with his head half turned round, watched him out of the
corner of his little grey eye with a look of extreme suspicion
and distrust. The drover observed this, and knowing perhaps
the influence of this individual, addressed him particularly in
accents of such seductive blarney as would have melted the
heart of anything but a pig. The shrewd old hog however was
not to be gammoned. At the conclusion of the address he gave
a short dry grunt, which was taken up and echoed in different
cadences by the rest of the drove. It resembled very much the
ironical cries of " hear," by which Hon. Members of the House
of Commons express their scornful contempt for anything
addressed by a political opponent. The drover was puzzled. It
was enough to make a saint swear. He, being a sinner, swore
outrageously. He damned them in all the moods and tenses,

and consigned them body and soul to a worse place than the slaughter house. "Bad luck to yez," continued he, "if yez won't listen to reason take this," and he forthwith proceeded to administer the lash with great impartiality. Immediately, the drove wheeled about with a shrill squeal of defiance, and rushing forward upset their conductor and swept the pier like a hurricane carrying dismay wherever they went. However these " Exiles of Erin " were all ultimately collected and put on board.

Here endeth my log rather abruptly.